BUSINESS IN A CHANGING CLIMATE

Explaining Industry Support for Carbon Pricing

Business in a Changing Climate

Explaining Industry Support for Carbon Pricing

KAIJA BELFRY MUNROE

UNIVERSITY OF TORONTO PRESS
Toronto Buffalo London

ISBN 978-1-4875-0055-9

Library and Archives Canada Cataloguing in Publication

Munroe, Kaija Belfry, 1981–, author
Business in a changing climate : explaining industry support for carbon pricing / Kaija Belfry Munroe.

Includes bibliographical references.
ISBN 978-1-4875-0055-9 (cloth)

1. Carbon taxes – Economic aspects.   2. Climatic changes – Government policy.   3. Industries – Environmental aspects.   I. Title.

HD2753.A3M85   2016   363.738'746   C2016-905831-X

University of Toronto Press acknowledges the financial assistance to its publishing program of the Canada Council for the Arts and the Ontario Arts Council, an agency of the Government of Ontario.

Canada Council   Conseil des Arts
for the Arts   du Canada

ONTARIO ARTS COUNCIL
CONSEIL DES ARTS DE L'ONTARIO
an Ontario government agency
un organisme du gouvernement de l'Ontario

Funded by the   Financé par le
Government   gouvernement
of Canada   du Canada

Contents

BUSINESS IN A CHANGING CLIMATE

Explaining Industry Support for Carbon Pricing

Chapter One

Introduction

It was a rather unexpected response. On 7 January 2008, Canada's National Round Table on the Environment and the Economy (NRTEE) released a report on climate change calling for government to implement "an economy-wide emission price policy" (NRTEE 2007). As the politically indecorous term "carbon tax" began appearing in the headlines of all of Canada's major news outlets, the political class – both government and opposition – responded with derision. In this context, swift condemnation from industry could only be expected. After all, a carbon price was anticipated to increase the costs of production in Canada. Yet despite the business community's history of campaigning against climate change action, particularly the Kyoto Protocol, no such condemnation came from Canada's major business associations or large firms.

On the contrary, the Canadian Council of Chief Executives (CCCE) – the voice of big business in Canada – was unambiguous in its support, calling the report "a sound and comprehensive policy blueprint" (CCCE 2008). Even more surprising, the Canadian Association of Petroleum Producers (CAPP) signalled cautious agreement, suggesting that its members were "ready to move" on the policy (Cheadle 2008). This left the federal government to oppose its own advisory board and the public to wonder what was going on in climate politics in Canada.

Why would two of Canada's largest business associations come out in favour of a policy instrument whose purpose is to increase their members' costs? Did other associations and firms agree with this stance, or are these groups an anomaly among economic actors in Canada? Why and when did these associations shift their climate change policy preference away from the voluntary programs and subsidies to which they had been committed for over a decade? How can one explain this puzzling turn of events in Canadian environmental politics?

These questions are significant, as they point to an under-researched area of Canadian and, indeed, global political economy: the public policy preferences of major firms and business associations. Scholars in Canada and elsewhere have argued that "big business" has considerable, if variable, influence over public policy outcomes (see, for instance, Doern 1978; Mansbridge 1992; Toner and Doern 1986; Vogel 1989). If this is indeed so, then what business wants, and why, has a significant impact on Canadian politics. In this case, however, not only is it uncertain what climate change policy instruments the Canadian business community supports; it remains unclear how and why it developed these preferences in the first place. The easiest explanation – that business groups look to the cost of compliance in determining their climate change policy instrument preferences – does not appear to provide an explanation of the case.

Upon further examination, the puzzle only deepens. In 2008 I conducted interviews on business preferences for climate change policy instruments with executives at all of Canada's heavy-emitting industry associations and a selection of large firms from the cement, forestry, and oil and gas sectors. CAPP's and CCCE's support for carbon pricing did not represent an anomaly in the business community in 2008 and 2009. Of the thirty business associations and large firms that participated in the survey, twenty-seven declared strong support for carbon pricing.

There was, however, variation in the type of carbon price they supported. Four associations and seven firms stated an explicit preference for cap-and-trade, and although only CAPP preferred a modified form of carbon taxation, four firms articulated a clear preference for that instrument. Moreover, of the five firms and seven associations that had no official preference for a particular type of carbon price, representatives at four associations and one firm articulated "unofficial" or personal support for taxation. This is interesting, as it suggests greater support for taxation among industry executives than would otherwise be apparent. Finally, although there was overwhelming support for carbon pricing in 2008–09, it seems that preference was relatively new. Representatives of firms and associations traced their preferences back to 2006–07, when the Canadian business community appears to have overwhelmingly shifted its support away from voluntary agreements and subsidies to carbon pricing. Table 1 lists the preferences of participating firms and associations in the study.

Table 1. Preferences for Carbon Pricing, Selected Industry Associations and Firms, Canada, 2009

Association or Firm	Supports Carbon Pricing?	Official Preference	Unofficial (Personal) Preference
Canadian Electricity Association	No	Time, money (through increase in price where regulated)	
Mining Association of Canada	Yes	None	Carbon tax
Canadian Vehicle Manufacturers' Association	Yes	Cap-and-trade	
Canadian Steel Producers Association	Yes	None	No
Canadian Gas Association	Yes	None	Carbon tax
Encana	Yes	Carbon tax	
Union Gas	Yes	Carbon tax	
Gaz Métro	Yes	Cap-and-trade	
Canadian Petroleum Products Institute	Yes	None	Carbon tax
Canadian Council of Chief Executives	Yes	None	Carbon tax
Canadian Chemical Producers' Association	Yes	Cap-and-trade	
Railway Association of Canada	Yes	Cap-and-trade	
Forest Products Association of Canada	Yes	None	Cap-and-trade
Weyerhaeuser	Yes	Cap-and-trade	
Canfor	Yes	None	Cap-and-trade
Catalyst Paper	Yes	None	Carbon tax
West Fraser Timber	Yes	None	No
AbitibiBowater	Yes	Cap-and-trade	
Aluminum Association of Canada	Yes	Cap-and-trade	
Canadian Association of Petroleum Producers (CAPP)	Yes	Modified carbon tax	
ConocoPhillips Canada	Yes	Carbon tax in Canada (cap-and-trade in United States)	
Suncor Energy	Yes	Cap-and-trade	
Nexen	Yes	Carbon tax	
Petro-Canada	Unclear	None (but supported CAPP position)	No
Shell Canada	Yes	Cap-and-trade	
Cement Association of Canada	Yes	None	
Essroc	Qualified	Voluntary/carbon tax	
St. Mary's Cement	Yes	Cap-and-trade	
Holcim Canada	Yes	Cap-and-trade	
Lehigh Cement	Yes	None	Cap-and-trade

Notes: The table shows official preferences formally adopted by the association or firm through its decision-making apparatus; in many cases, however, representatives from associations or firms with no official preference articulated unofficial or personal support for an instrument. The Canadian Association of Petroleum Producers supported a carbon tax on marginal emissions above a set quota, unlike traditional carbon taxation, which would tax all emissions. Essroc did declare its support for carbon pricing, if necessary, but its first preference was for voluntary agreements. Petro-Canada's official views on carbon pricing were contradictory, and thus no preference is recorded.

These three empirical findings – that Canadian business overwhelmingly supported carbon pricing in 2009, that there was considerable variation in the type of price supported, and that there was a shift in aggregate business preference in 2006–07 – raise the (research) question: *What causes variation in business preferences for climate change policy instruments over time and among firms and industry associations?*

Ultimately, business preferences for climate change policy instruments are based on assessments of the risks and advantages of particular policy instruments, and expectations about future government policy instrument choices and their impacts on the firm strongly influence these assessments. Expectations, in turn, are influenced by the political context of the day and by previous experience with a policy instrument. As these factors change, therefore, so do business preferences for climate change policy instruments.

The Methods

This argument, summarized in the form of the model I present below, was developed inductively from interview data and a review of the risk management literature. The study began with a deductive methodology, as is normal practice in political science: five hypotheses (see Chapter 2), based on a range of scholarly literatures, were to be tested against the findings of a qualitative and comparative research design. Unfortunately, not long into the interview process, it became clear that, although many of these hypotheses appeared to have some relevance, none could explain the puzzle entirely. Moreover, interview subjects pointed to a missing variable – risk – that emerged as the link between each of the other seemingly unrelated explanatory variables.

During the interview process, I also undertook a review of the popular and scholarly risk management literature. As most of this literature is pragmatic in purpose (how can managers mitigate risk?), rather than analytical (what effects do a focus on risk management have on firm decisions?), the utility of this literature was largely in expanding the explanations (and particularly the definitions) provided by the interview subjects themselves.

At this stage, I had a problem: the question (the observed variation in business preferences) and the answer (the model) were largely developed from the same data (interviews). Clearly, interpretation was required, but how could I know that my interpretations were correct? George and Bennett (2005) argue that, in such a case, the researcher should develop a secondary test of the model within the same case, using new data and falsifiable observations. The researcher can then feel confident that the model is internally consistent and indeed provides a strong explanation of the particular case under investigation. This is the method I followed, and the findings of that secondary process are laid out in Chapters 4 through 8. Scholarly readers interested in a deeper discussion of the methods and their foundation in the literature are encouraged to turn to Chapter 3; those wanting to avoid such a discussion should feel free to skip it.

The Argument

The central argument of this book has two parts. First, business preferences for climate change policy instruments are developed not only with an eye to limiting compliance costs, but also to limiting the *risk* created by the policy instrument (with respect to both the firm's own capital investments and investment in the firm by external investors), while optimizing any possible advantage. Risk here is defined as uncertainty that an investment will receive the expected return; the concept highlights the significance of predictability and the stability of costs, rather than just the absolute level of costs associated with an instrument. I discuss the significance of this change in language – from cost to risk – in greater detail below.

Second, as these assessments are made in the context of considerable uncertainty – with regard both to which policy instruments are likely to be implemented *and* to the design and impact of any policy instrument once implemented – they are strongly influenced by managerial and investor expectations about future government policy instrument choices. For instance, is it probable that government will implement a cap-and-trade program? If so, which industries will be covered? Will the cap be high or low? Will the market price be stable or volatile? Expectations related to these sorts of questions are not created in a vacuum. Rather, the political context, particularly public attention, strongly influences expectations about which policy instruments might be implemented, while previous firm experience with a policy instrument influences expectations about the costs associated with a particular instrument and the predictability of those costs. The following model summarizes this two-part argument.

The Risk-Advantage Model of Business Policy Preferences

Overall, in determining preferences for particular policy instruments, business decision-makers attempt to:

1) limit risk to the company created by the policy instrument in the firm's *own capital investments*;
2) limit the effects of the policy instrument on the risk perceptions of *external investors*; and
3) seek *advantage* from the policy instrument where possible.

Assessments of risk and advantage are undertaken in the context of considerable uncertainty both about the likelihood of an instrument's being implemented *and* the design details and impacts of that instrument. Consequently, expectations play a key role in determining perceptions of risk and advantage. Those expectations are based on:

4) the *political context* (likelihood of implementation); and
5) the firm's *past experience* with a policy instrument (design details and impacts).

RISK AND ADVANTAGE

Readers from the social sciences might find this book's definition of risk surprising. The conceptualization of risk as uncertainty that an investment will receive its expected return is, however, commonplace in management and business administration, the fields most familiar to the business elite. Indeed, this definition best fits the usage employed by interview subjects in this study. In addition, although many academic definitions of risk differentiate between quantifiable risk and non-quantifiable uncertainty (Knight 1985), the definition I use makes no such differentiation. Rather, risk is here defined as a particular type of uncertainty, whether quantifiable or not, an added nuance that again matches usage of the term by the interview subjects. Finally, although some disciplines also view risk as relating to the potential for positive or negative outcomes (upside versus downside risk) (Hubbard 2009), the interview subjects appeared to perceive risk as a purely negative phenomenon. Managers were concerned that they would receive less than the expected return on investment. That they could receive more did not cause concern – indeed, this was generally called an advantage, opportunity, or benefit. In this book, therefore, the term risk relates to negative potentialities.

Clearly, the concept of risk incorporates the influence of cost. In order to protect long-term returns on investment and ensure that they reach the expected level, managers must attempt to limit the costs associated with production, including those created by regulation. However, the concept of risk highlights the significance of cost predictability and stability. In other words, in attempting to increase the certainty related to *expected* returns, it is equally important that costs be determined in advance, a requirement that, it was found, was actually more important than keeping costs below some absolute value. In deciding which of two policy instruments to support, a firm might actually prefer the more costly of the two if it is more likely to provide long-term cost stability. Indeed, the importance of cost stability and predictability versus the absolute level of costs is why managers interviewed for this study differentiated between risk and cost. As Avrim Lazar, president of the Forest Products Association of Canada (FPAC), put it, "cost minimization is not my number one priority. My number one priority is risk minimization."

The significance of risk also highlights the significance of *policy certainty* in influencing business preferences for climate change policy instruments. Again, as risk is a type of uncertainty, decreasing the risk associated with climate change policy instruments is ultimately about decreasing uncertainty within the regulatory realm. Although the design details of a particular policy instrument theoretically might create greater or lesser predictability of cost, it is impossible to have cost stability if a government continually changes or threatens to change the regulatory regime. Firms need to be able to predict the long-term impacts of regulation on their investments, so a vacillating government can be one of the greatest impediments to investment and, ultimately, to business success.

The investment definition of risk also highlights another significant point included in the model. Firms examine the potential for risk created by a policy instrument from two perspectives: in relation to the firm's own capital investments and in relation to the investments made by external investors in the firm itself. In the former case, the firm attempts to determine the likelihood that the policy instrument will create uncertainty about the returns on its plants, factories, and other investments. For instance, if a carbon tax were implemented at $40 per tonne, would a new processing plant still provide an acceptable return? In the latter case, a firm that grapples with the risk perceptions of external investors is confronted by the possibility that shareholders or creditors will withhold funds due to uncertainty over expected returns caused by the potential implementation of the policy instrument. Do investors believe they will receive their expected return if the aforementioned carbon tax is implemented? Even the possibility of such a regulatory change might spook jittery investors.

Investors, whether within or without the firm, base their investment decisions on a trade-off between risk and return, meaning that higher levels of risk without corresponding increases in expected returns would undermine investment. Attempting to anticipate and allay investor risk perceptions, however, requires keeping one eye on the firm's reputation and public image. The Canadian regulatory environment does not allow most investors access to inside information, so they must base their assessments on publicly available information (Hall and Soskice 2003). Ultimately, the risk perceptions of capital investors and shareholders are important for two reasons. First, without large capital investments, the firm would have difficulty growing and competing; second, if shareholders perceive the risks of investing as too high, they might sell their stock, leading to depressed share prices and increased likelihood of hostile acquisition by a competitor (Martin and McConnell 1981; Powell 1997). Clearly, both possibilities would adversely impact the long-term success and survival of the firm (and its current management) and, therefore, firms form preferences for policy instruments that would mitigate against these potentialities (the least "risky" instruments).

Some readers nonetheless might view the shift of terminology from cost to risk as solely semantic. After all, a more nuanced understanding of cost would incorporate many of the components discussed above. I argue, however, that this shift is necessary in order to clarify how, why, and for what purpose large firms interact with government. The focus on risk takes uncertainty seriously, and highlights the fact that firms will respond to environmental policy in a manner that takes into account norms of appropriateness. Although it is easy to assume, when scholars refer to cost mitigation in relation to corporate lobbying, that absolute cost levels are the key determinant of a firm's action vis-à-vis government, in reality the need for cost predictability and stability, as well as the need to mitigate external investor concerns, might well trump absolute cost considerations. The focus on risk brings this fact to the forefront of discussion.

On the other side of the ledger, advantage is defined as the firm's capacity to increase revenue as a result of the implementation of a policy instrument. This could be directly through the policy instrument's design or indirectly by changing the behaviour of key customers in the market. What is important is that the instrument is viewed as strengthening the firm's position either in absolute terms (more revenue or reputational gains) or in relative terms vis-à-vis competitors.

EXPECTATIONS

The second element of the model – that managers' expectations about future government policy choices and their effects on the firm strongly influence perceptions of risk and advantage – also requires some explanation. In seeking to limit risks and optimize advantages in creating preferences for climate change policy instruments, firms are attempting to control the effects of government actions on their investments in an uncertain future. Their expectations about that future, therefore, impact how they perceive the risks and advantages. Two types of expectations matter. First, firms seek a stable, certain regulatory environment in which to invest and, therefore, their expectations about the likelihood of regulatory change and the implementation of a particular policy instrument influence their perceptions of risk. Only once there is an expectation of regulatory change does the regulatory environment become uncertain and thus risky, and once that happens, only those instruments that conceivably could be implemented – providing a new, stable regulatory regime – require attention. For instance, a government conceivably could nationalize all oil companies as a response to climate change, but if that has never been debated in the public discourse, it would not be considered a significant possibility. Expectations about changes in the regulatory environment thus encompass both the likelihood of change and the probable direction of that change.

Second, expectations about the impacts of a policy instrument on the firm are also significant, and these are influenced by previous experience with an instrument. Although the political context influences expectations about regulatory change and about which instruments are likely to be implemented, it cannot explain all firm preferences. Some instruments – nationalization, for instance – might be "off the table," but there is often more than one option under public discussion at a time. If both a carbon tax and a cap-and-trade program are equally likely, how do firms choose? An expert analysis of the costs associated with particular policy instruments might indicate a clear choice, but my research found that firms did not necessarily support an instrument solely on that basis. Indeed, it was only once the firm had experienced a policy instrument (in another jurisdiction) that those arguments were certain to hold sway. Once the firm experienced a particular policy instrument, its effects were viewed as known or certain and less risky than the alternatives. Thus, in the absence of experience, managers were more likely to discount expert evaluations of costs and the predictability of costs; where a firm had experience with a policy instrument, its managers all but invariably preferred it to likely alternatives.

Climate Change Policy Instruments and the Theoretical Cost of Compliance

The preceding analysis raises two questions. First, what are climate change policy instruments? Second, what is the expert advice with respect to the costs associated with each instrument? With respect to the first question, in this book I use three different terms to refer to the public policy process. First, by *policy*, I refer to the "broad framework of ideas and values within which decisions are taken and action, or inaction, is pursued by governments in relation to some issue or problem" (Brooks 1989, 16). Policy includes both goals and means. Climate policy, for example, specifies a *policy goal* vis-à-vis climate change – namely, to reduce the emission of greenhouse gases, notably carbon dioxide, often by a specific amount or to a particular target.

Second, the public policy process also refers to the means or mechanisms – called *policy instruments* – by which that goal is to be achieved. Indeed, *environmental policy instruments* can be defined as the tools through which governments "wield their power in attempting to affect society – in terms of values and beliefs, action and organization – in such a way as to improve, or to prevent the deterioration of, the quality of the natural environment" (Mickwitz 2003, 419). I focus specifically on environmental policy instruments developed to mitigate climate change, which might vary significantly in terms of their coerciveness and/or the costs they create for firms or consumers.

Finally, by the *regulatory environment*, I refer to the total set of policy instruments, rules, and legislation within which businesses operate – everything from payroll taxes to local zoning rules that determine where certain business activities may be undertaken. This could also be called the political economy (Hall and Soskice 2003). From the firm's perspective, the regulatory environment is a key determinant of both short- and long-run costs; if these costs are unpredictable, returns on investment both by and in the firm become uncertain. Thus, potential changes to policy instruments within the regulatory environment create risks to such investments. Climate change policy instruments are only one possible source of such risks.

The distinction between policy goals and policy instruments (or means) is an important one because it is often blurred in discussions about climate change. Once a government has established a policy goal of, say, reducing carbon emissions by a specific amount, it could in principle employ one of a range of policy instruments to bring about that reduction. Different policy instruments tend to be considered as linked to different policy goals, however, precisely because they vary in terms of cost and coerciveness. A government with an ambitious target for reductions might find that its policy goal is not credible if it pursues these reductions through, for example, voluntary agreements. Conversely, different policy instruments might be associated implicitly with different reduction targets (that is, different policy goals). As these implicit assumptions are both empirically elusive and heavily dependent on context, I assume that a firm develops preferences about policy instruments on their own merits, rather than on beliefs about what those instruments imply about specific policy goals; for instance, a government might impose a lower target if it employed a carbon tax rather than a cap-and-trade system. Nothing in the research – in my interviews or in other data – implies that this assumption is invalid or that this sort of strategic lobbying plays a central role in the development of policy instrument preferences. Nonetheless, in some cases – with respect to voluntary agreements, for instance – a policy instrument might provide leeway for a firm to influence government policy goals, and I take this into account in the discussion of costs below. Otherwise, however, I assume that climate change policy instrument preferences and government policy goals are independent.

What policy instruments are particularly related to climate change policy, and what are the costs associated with each? I have already mentioned cap-and-trade programs and carbon taxes, but these are not the only possible instruments: In fact, five climate change policy instruments are available to governments. Four of these can be ordered in terms of their theoretical costs to business to achieve the same policy goal, from least costly to most costly: 1) subsidies; 2) voluntary agreements; 3) grandfathered cap-and-trade systems (emissions trading without an initial auction of allowances); and 4) traditional carbon taxation. If, for the purpose of this discussion, one assumes that firms prefer less costly policy instruments, this list should also represent their order of preference for climate change policy instruments.

The fifth policy instrument, traditional "command-and-control" regulation, is somewhat outside this traditional preference ordering.

This is because the lack of alternatives to mitigation, the legal imperatives inherent in the system (compared with all other instruments), and the difficulty a firm might have in meeting these standards in the context of climate change mean that the costs of traditional regulation are difficult to compare with those of other policy instruments. It is likely, therefore, that traditional regulation would be the least popular policy instrument; however, as I discuss in greater detail below, a firm might prefer regulation to taxation if it believes it can meet the required standards while keeping the per unit cost of doing so (or paying the penalty for failing to do so) less than or equivalent to the tax.[1] The threat of unknown legal penalty if it fails to meet the standards, however, makes this proposition very risky.

The level of coercion entailed by the policy instrument, thus also affects the ordering of preferences. From the firm's perspective, the first two policy instruments – subsidies and voluntary agreements – can be considered types of voluntary programs, as the firm would not *generally* be forced to take part in these initiatives. Cap-and-trade programs, taxation, and command-and-control regulation, on the other hand, can all be seen from the firm's perspective as forms of regulation, since firms covered under these programs do not have a choice whether or not to participate but are compelled to comply with their rules, which are enforced through some form of penalty, either financial or legal. Although this dichotomy represents an oversimplification of policy instruments – subsidies can be compulsory, voluntary agreements can be undertaken under threat of regulation, and so on – the firms in this study perceived the instruments in this manner; they were, after all, creating preferences based on general understandings of instruments without information of particular details or exceptions to these rules.

Unsurprisingly, perhaps, all things being equal, voluntary programs are far less costly for the firm than regulatory instruments. Subsidies are by far the cheapest policy instrument for the firm, as all or most of the cost is incurred by the state (Field and Olewiler 1994). Voluntary agreements are the second-best scenario for the firm. They provide considerable leeway for industry to negotiate lower abatement levels

---

1 The firm might meet the standard under command-and-control and pay no further
   tax; under carbon taxation, the firm could mitigate until paying the tax was cheaper
   and then pay the tax on all further emissions.

(ensuring lower costs), as well as opportunities to influence positive public perceptions of their environmental and social conscience (Arora and Cason 1996; Harrison and Antweiler 2003). Voluntary agreements also provide significant flexibility for the firm to design its abatement strategies based on the least costly options.

Cap-and-trade systems typically are the third-cheapest instrument for the firm. In this regulatory system, a government sets a cap on the quantity of emissions allowed in the entire economy and then provides emissions allowances to existing firms up to that total capped amount under some form of allocation formula – based, for example, on past emissions, the average for the industry, and so on. As the cap likely would be lower than the current quantity of emissions, a firm generally would need to reduce its emissions. In doing so, it would have three choices: it could lower emissions to a point equal to its original allocation; it could lower emissions to a point less than its original allocation and sell its remaining allowances to other firms for a price higher than the cost per unit of reduction – its "marginal cost of abatement" – or it could lower emissions to a point greater than its original allocation and then buy credits from another firm at a price lower than its marginal cost of abatement.

Again, assuming that an existing firm's allowances are "grandfathered" into the process – meaning it need not buy its original allowances from the government – a cap-and-trade system allows a firm the flexibility to lower the total cost of its emissions reduction that is unavailable under a strict emissions standard that is uniform across firms. This is generally possible because firms have different marginal costs of emissions abatement, and thus both buyers and sellers are better off from the transaction. Unsurprisingly, a study of the US sulphur oxides and nitrogen oxides cap-and-trade system confirms that this instrument provides significant cost savings to industry compared with traditional regulation (Burtraw and Palmer 2004).

All else being equal – in other words, assuming that the tax set by government is similar to the market-derived price in an emissions trading system – a tax typically is a far more expensive policy instrument for the firm than, for example, a grandfathered cap-and-trade system in which the firm would pay only for emissions above a certain limit. As the tax would be imposed on all of a firm's emissions, not merely on those that exceed a set quota, a firm would pay the tax on emissions and any costs of mitigation it might choose to undertake. It therefore would make sense for the firm to reduce its emissions until its marginal cost of emissions abatement was equal to the tax, at which point paying the tax would become cost-effective. This approach, of course, assumes that reductions are technologically feasible, which is not necessarily the case for all carbon emissions.

As stated above, traditional command-and-control regulation is harder to pin down when it comes to a cost-based preference ordering. Conceivably, since the firm would have to mitigate only those emissions above a set standard – based on either emissions or technology – command-and-control might be cheaper than taxation, which would require the firm to pay tax on *all* non-mitigated emissions. This policy instrument, however, makes the key assumption that mitigation is both possible *and* not cost-prohibitive. With respect to emissions, if a firm were unable to meet the standard – because, for instance, with current technology, this is not possible at current levels of output or because the technology required is cost-prohibitive – it might have no choice but to shut down operations to avoid a legal or financial penalty in addition to the reputational costs of non-compliance. With respect to technology, a firm might be required to adopt something costly – indeed, conceivably far more costly than any probable tax. Needless to say, it would be hard for the firm to compare the costs of a command-and-control regulatory framework and those of a taxation mechanism without the details of both programs. However, since taxation would provide an "out" for a firm that faced high mitigation costs (paying the tax), while command-and-control regulation would impose a penalty only for non-compliance, such a firm would be expected to prefer taxation to command-and-control.

In reality, of course, the details of any climate change policy instrument could be expected to affect business costs, and thus might affect the ordering of preferences. Most significantly, original credit allocations for a cap-and-trade program could be sold or auctioned, not grandfathered. In that case, a firm would be forced to pay not only for its emissions above the cap, but also for the original allocation. Consequently, the costs of an auctioned cap-and-trade system would be comparable to those of a carbon tax.

Although taxation appears to be less appealing to industry than grandfathered cap-and-trade, revenue-neutral taxation – whereby government gains no extra revenue from the policy instrument – might be easier to accept. If a firm believed that all or most of the tax would be returned through other tax reductions, cost expectations would differ greatly from those of traditional taxation. A firm could decrease its overall taxation level through pollution abatement measures until its marginal cost of abatement was equal to the tax rate; it could then expect a significant amount of the remaining tax to be counteracted by tax decreases in other areas. Thus, in this theoretical situation, the firm would expect to pay the price of mitigation plus the non-counteracted tax. The exact cost would depend on the details of the revenue-neutrality arrangement.

There is, however, no guarantee that the tax would be returned to the firm through other sources – a tax on emissions could be used, for example, to reduce personal income tax, which would provide no relief to the firm. Such a tax would be revenue-neutral, but from the perspective of government, rather than that of the firm or industry. As well, even if tax collected from a given industry is returned to that industry, inequalities related to the distribution of funds within the industry – which firms receive how much – could create conflict among firms. It is possible that a revenue-neutral carbon tax could be developed such that some firms would be better off than under a grandfathered cap-and-trade system – that is, if they pay little carbon tax because their carbon intensity is low *and* they benefit substantially from the corporate tax cuts determined by government. However, at least as many firms likely would find themselves on the losing end of such an arrangement. Moreover, and most important, it would be impossible for firms to know the exact cost of a revenue-neutral tax (the tax paid minus the tax reduced) in advance, meaning that even the "winning" firms in that scenario would not know that they were winners before the details of the program were set by government. Revenue neutrality, therefore, introduces considerable uncertainty into the cost of a carbon tax.

There are other areas of uncertainty related to the costs of particular instruments. A cap-and-trade program, in particular, requires government to make decisions about a range of variables, including the level of the cap, the base year upon which the initial allocation will be made, which industries to regulate, whether to include offsets from non-regulated industries, and whether the program will be "economy-wide" – that is, whether it will include unregulated emissions by changing the location of regulation to producers, rather than users, of fossil fuels. All these variables can be expected to affect not just the costs to a firm of a cap-and-trade program, but also the competitive position of some firms in relation to others. Moreover, even once the program is developed and the details are set, the market price for emissions allowances also might be quite unpredictable, creating another significant area of uncertainty about the costs of the program. Finally, transaction costs associated with buying and selling within the new market – fees from banks, lawyers, and other brokers – introduce further cost uncertainty. Thus, although a grandfathered cap-and-trade program likely would be the lowest-cost regulatory option for firms, compared with taxation or traditional regulation, the complexity of program design and the fact that the price would be market determined makes predicting the absolute value of those costs challenging. With respect to command-and-control regulation, variables that might affect a firm's costs include lead-in time (the time that firms are given to prepare), the level of penalties, the breadth of coverage (who will be regulated), the stringency of coverage for existing versus new plants or firms, and the basis of the standard – for example, it might require firms to employ best-in-class or the most efficient technology or meet particular environmental goals.

Despite these uncertainties, one can draw two key points from this analysis. First, voluntary instruments (voluntary agreements and subsidies) can be expected to be far less costly to a firm than any regulatory instruments (cap-and-trade, taxation, or traditional regulation). Second, of the carbon-pricing instruments, a grandfathered cap-and-trade program can be expected to be considerably less expensive to a firm than a traditional carbon tax, since the firm would pay only for emissions above a set quota in the former scenario and on all emissions in the latter. Revenue neutrality complicates this analysis, making it possible that some firms would be better off under a carbon tax. It would be difficult, however, for a firm to know in advance if it would be among the "winners" in the revenue-neutrality lottery, as this would be highly dependent on the politically determined details of the program. That return would not only be uncertain; it would also need to be substantial to make up the difference in cost between carbon taxation and grandfathered cap-and-trade. Thus, preferring a revenue-neutral carbon tax to a grandfathered cap-and-trade program on the grounds that it might entail lower costs to the firm for the same policy goal would represent a considerable gamble.

These two points highlight two key questions related to the empirical findings of this study. First, why did Canadian firms shift their preferences away from voluntary agreements and subsidies towards carbon pricing in 2006–07? Second, what explains the variation in preferences for carbon-pricing mechanisms observed after this shift? Although arguments can be made in favour of either policy instrument – grandfathered cap-and-trade can offer lower costs more predictably, while traditional carbon taxation offers greater price certainty – why do some firms and associations support a grandfathered cap-and-trade program while others support taxation or have no preference? It can be assumed that the lack of a clear preference on the part of many associations is due to the internal machinations of the organization and the lack of a homogeneous view among its member firms, but this is itself puzzling: why is there such variation in preferences for climate change policy instruments even within the same sector?

Certainly, a simple account of preferences based on relative costs of compliance cannot answer these questions. This is both because the variation in preferences is far more diverse than such an analysis would predict – the only aspect born out in reality was that firms were indeed averse to command-and-control regulation – and because the true costs associated with carbon-pricing instruments are complex and uncertain. The risk-advantage model, however, offers insight into both puzzling findings, explaining why there was a shift in aggregate business preference in 2006–07 away from voluntary initiatives and how and why firms and associations developed their particular carbon-pricing preferences thereafter.

Why Did Business Shift Preferences away from Voluntary Agreements and Subsidies?

The Canadian business community shifted its preferences away from the less costly voluntary agreements and subsidies because firms and their investors began to expect that government would abandon voluntary policy instruments, thus no longer giving firms and investors the long-term policy certainty they require to facilitate investment. As risk is a type of uncertainty, seeking to minimize risk in the regulatory realm ultimately means that, all else being equal, firms prefer policy instruments that provide long-term policy certainty. Policy certainty, however, has two dimensions. On the one hand, firms seek regulatory *stability* – the knowledge that the regulatory environment will remain unchanged throughout the lifespan of an investment. On the other hand, they also seek policy instruments that provide *predictability* of costs and revenues. This does not negate the importance of limiting compliance costs related to policy instruments, but it highlights the fact that the theoretical cost of a particular policy instrument might be less important than the ability to predict the costs associated with the regulatory environment over the long term.

Usually, the status quo regulatory environment provides the greatest possible certainty from the perspective of both stability and predictability. The details of that environment are known and have been experienced, and the costs they create are predictable. If a firm is succeeding in this environment, it would prefer the status quo to continue over the long term, and would support only relatively minor changes or those deemed to provide advantage with relatively little risk. In Canada, from 1989 to 2006, business supported only voluntary agreements and subsidies, which involved only minor changes to the regulatory environment, were the least costly policy instruments, and offered considerable cost predictability, while providing some advantage in reputation and efficiency gains.

Once changes in the political environment create expectations of regulatory change, however, the status quo loses its stability and a key asset of the regulatory environment is lost. At this point, firms no longer can make long-term investment decisions predicated on the continuance of the current regulatory framework. Moreover, external investors who are aware of the potential for regulatory change will also perceive higher risk. They might respond, in the case of major capital investors, by refusing to provide funds for large projects or, in the case of shareholders, by moving their investments to less risky alternatives in different industries or jurisdictions. In the latter case, a drop in shareholder demand could lead to a drop in share price, which, in turn, could increase a firm's vulnerability to a hostile takeover. Ultimately, these adverse outcomes are a consequence of uncertainty about the future regulatory regime; it is the mere perception of the likelihood of change that causes this, not the nature of the future regime per se.

The significant negative effects of policy instability make managers extremely cognizant of the need for stability in the regulatory realm. Articulating preferences vis-à-vis policy instruments can be seen as an attempt to hasten the resolution of uncertainty created by expectations of regulatory change. Such preferences signal government that a firm wishes a particular instrument to be implemented, and help communicate to investors that the firm can assure acceptable returns on investment despite potential regulatory change. In Canada, following a shift in public opinion in 2006 and a political debate that privileged market-based mechanisms, firms and business associations abandoned their previous preference for voluntary agreements and subsidies, overwhelmingly adopted a preference for carbon pricing, and called for government to apply a price as soon as possible.

Why did Canadian firms respond so noticeably to a change in public opinion? A public opinion shift acts as a catalyst for a change in expectations that undermines perceived regulatory stability. In other words, the shift in public opinion indicated a new trend in Canadian public policy, and led managers to believe that the status quo could no longer be trusted to continue throughout the lifespan of investments and that government ultimately would respond by implementing a carbon price. Public opinion also had the added effect of ensuring that investors – whether major investment firms with staff tasked with cataloguing risks or retail shareholders who make choices based on far less information – were well aware of this trend. Once climate change rose to the forefront of the public policy agenda, thus creating uncertainty about the future regulatory environment and therefore risks to investment, investor concern became a motivating factor for firms' policy instrument preferences.

Public opinion thus plays a dual role in policy preference development: it highlights areas of likely regulatory change *and* it acts as an indicator of investor concern for firms. With respect to the latter point, investors are a diverse and disparate group, but what they have in common is that they are a subset of the wider public – the investor class, so to speak – and the same political forces that shape public opinion also shape their perceptions of risk within the regulatory realm. For firms trying to control and assuage perceptions of risk on the part of investors, therefore, public opinion provides a handy indicator of investor concern.

Why Does Support for Carbon-Pricing Instruments Vary?

In the Canadian case, as Table 1 demonstrates, firms and associations overwhelmingly declared their support for a carbon price after public opinion in 2006–07 demanded action. They could not agree, however, on whether they ought to support a grandfathered cap-and-trade program or a revenue-neutral carbon tax.[2] Why this variation? The risk-advantage model suggests that the explanation lies in the interaction of two variables: advantage and experience.

As noted earlier, four associations and seven firms supported a grandfathered cap-and-trade program, the option most likely to entail lower costs. Eight firms and eight associations, however, all of which

---

2 At the time, it was widely assumed that any cap-and-trade program would be grandfathered and, although there was some variation, most respondents also assumed that a carbon tax would be revenue neutral.

supported carbon pricing in general, either preferred a carbon tax or had no clear preference. Thus, even though, for most firms, a grandfathered cap-and-trade program likely would be cheaper than a carbon tax, depending on neutrality arrangements, a majority of participating firms and associations did not endorse that policy instrument.

The risk-advantage model implies, however, that absolute costs are not the only determinant of business preferences. The concept of risk highlights the significance of cost stability and predictability for firms and, in this regard, a carbon tax is far superior to a grandfathered cap-and-trade program. Once government sets a carbon tax, firms are able to predict their costs over a relatively long time frame; in an emissions-trading system, in contrast, the carbon price could vary daily, if not hourly, and so is far more difficult to predict. A puzzling aspect of the findings remains, however: if price predictability is so important to firms, why do all firms and associations not support taxation? One could say that the need to ensure expected returns on investments (to limit risk) forces firms to trade off the lower costs offered by a grandfathered cap-and-trade program against the greater price predictability offered by a carbon tax. Certainly, interview subjects that supported a grandfathered cap-and-trade program tended to highlight the flexibility and lower costs associated with that policy instrument, while those that supported a carbon tax tended to highlight price predictability and deride the uncertainty in costs associated with cap-and-trade. Such an explanation, however, does not clarify why some firms valued price predictability while others valued lower cost. Clearly, an intervening variable is at work when firms choose to lobby for one carbon-pricing instrument over another.

In an ideal world, firms would prefer policy instruments that kept costs both low and predictable. When – as it did in Canada from 2006 to 2009 – the political context pushes firms to choose between instruments that offer either cost predictability or lower cost, past experience plays a strong role in shaping this choice. Combined with perceived advantage, experience offers a far better explanation of the data than absolute considerations of either level or predictability of cost. Why?

Decision-makers with previous experience of an instrument at their firm viewed the arguments in favour of that instrument as more certainly correct and, therefore, compelling than those with no such experience, or experience with an alternative instrument. The numbers prove the point: of the nine firms with experience in cap-and-trade, six supported the instrument. Of the eight firms without experience in cap-and-trade, preferences varied: two supported a carbon tax, four had no preference, and two supported cap-and-trade. Despite the considerably lower costs that cap-and-trade entails, only two firms without experience with that instrument supported it. To mix metaphors, the devil is always in the details, and firms strongly preferred the devil they knew.

The important point here is to understand why experience matters so much to firms. I argue that experience has an ideational effect: familiarity with a policy instrument increases perceived certainty over design details and their impacts. Experience acts as a heuristic device: managers assume that the firm's previous experience with the policy instrument predicts future experience with it. In the absence of experience, decision-makers are left with competing arguments in favour of cap-and-trade or a carbon tax – either that the instrument is less costly or offers more predictable costs – and no clear way to choose between them. This lack of experience, moreover, breeds discomfort: since none of the details of potential instruments is certain, all are perceived as risky. With experience, however, details and effects are seen as more certain, and thus less risky, and managers give more credence to arguments in favour of it.

Two caveats are worth noting here. First, an overwhelmingly negative experience with an instrument can be expected to influence a firm's preferences in favour of some other instrument, since a negative outcome with that same instrument would be perceived as certain in the future. This helps explain why command-and-control regulation, despite its widespread use as a policy instrument, remains unpopular; the design of the system is based on the imposition of "sticks," rather than "carrots," and leaves little room for positive experience. With such an instrument, firms see only risk, in that, if they do not manage to decrease emissions to the set standard, they face an unknown penalty; moreover, they gain nothing for their success (and increased costs) other than the prevention of an even worse outcome in the form of the penalty. A similarly overwhelmingly negative experience with cap-and-trade led one cement company to oppose that policy instrument. Interestingly, however, where a policy instrument provided room for a positive experience (as with carbon-pricing instruments), firms were more likely than not to support the instrument they had experienced, rather than an instrument they had not, even if managers acknowledged some challenges or weaknesses of the previous experience. The *certainty* of survival and even growth under an experienced instrument appeared to decrease perceptions of risk in most cases, bolstering positive arguments in favour of an instrument and undermining negative views.

The second caveat is that, although I refer to managers' perspectives here, it should be kept in mind that the reference point for this discussion is the firm. That is, I assume that the firm had experience with a particular instrument for it to influence the firm's preferences going forward, even if a particular manager might have experienced another instrument with another firm. I assume, following Cyert and March (1993), that a firm's decisions are made in collectives or groups and, thus, that more than one individual's experience with a particular instrument would be needed for the firm to regard that experience as salient – although, in theory, a particular individual could act as a decision leader and transfer learning from one firm to another. Many questions, however, remain: which types of learning, if any, can transfer between firms? Which individuals can act as decision leaders? As the research design of my survey did not provide for answering these questions, I make the required assumption that experience must belong to the firm itself. Certainly, I uncovered no evidence to suggest this assumption is invalid, although further research is clearly required.

Although experience helps determine perceptions of risk, perceptions of advantage also influence policy instrument preferences. Firms that perceived a clear advantage in a policy instrument tended to support that instrument, even if they had no experience with it. Thus, I argue that variation in the type of carbon price supported is explained by variation in experience with carbon-pricing instruments and differences in perceived competitive advantage flowing from those instruments. Experience, however, appears to trump advantage, decreasing the significance of a clear competitive advantage where the two contradict. Where a firm had a theoretical advantage with one instrument (say, cap-and-trade), but experience in another (say, carbon taxation), it tended to have no official preference. In the end, business executives trust their own experience far more than they trust expert advice, and this tendency has a considerable impact on policy instrument preferences.

The Contributions

The central themes of this argument – that firms seek to reduce regulatory uncertainty in order to decrease risk, and that they seek advantage where possible – are hardly novel. Fundamental to economics and management understandings of corporate decision-making and profit is the effect of uncertainty (Hofmann 2007; Knight 1985; Power 2007), as well as investor/stakeholder concerns (Barnard 1991; Benn, Dunphy, and Martin 2009). Indeed, the term "political risk" found in any investment management textbook refers to the very concerns highlighted here: that changes in the political environment will undermine the capacity of investors to receive their expected return (Reilly and Brown 2006). Moreover, many of the central themes in this book are compatible with the findings of Gunningham, Kagan, and Thornton (2004), who asked why firms would adopt environmental practices in the absence of cost savings. They argue that firms were attempting to protect their "license to operate," which included social, economic, and regulatory demands from multiple stakeholders. Although policy instrument preferences must be kept analytically distinct from other corporate environmental action – because firms do not have direct control over whether their preferences are implemented in one case and complete control in the other – the authors also find that perceptions of environmental and regulatory risk influenced managers' decision-making on the environment.

The model presented here, therefore, does not reinvent the wheel; instead it helps to integrate components from a broad range of literatures that are elsewhere largely left separate, while providing explicit clarification about the decision-making process of business leaders vis-à-vis government policy instrument choice. Indeed, the particular area of interest here – firms' preferences for government policy instruments – has received limited specific attention in the literature, existing as it does at the intersection of political science, economics, and management. As a result, research into business-government relations often leaves firms' policy preferences undefined, and readers are left to infer what they will about what firms want from government and why they want it. Usually, the underlying assumption is that firms are attempting to minimize absolute costs – an assumption that, while correct in part, leaves out important nuance. Firms not only attempt to limit absolute costs; they also seek cost predictability and stability, and, where possible, advantage. Where these sometimes-conflicting goals do not indicate a clear preference, firms look to their own experience to fill the gap. I hope, therefore, that this study provides a foundation for further research into business-government relations in Canada, particularly the influence of business on the political process.

The study of business-government relations in Canada remains in its infancy, a state in which it has stagnated for a number of decades. As Bruce Doern, one of Canada's finest public policy scholars, stated in 1996, "Despite the excellent work of scholars such as Bill Coleman and some business historians, we still lack compelling studies of the power and policy influence of key firms and corporations, either in general or in particular policy domains." To this I would add that the study of business preferences for public policy, certainly a precursor to measuring the extent of its influence in public policy development, also remains largely underdeveloped. Only Douglas Macdonald's work on *Business and Environmental Politics in Canada* (2007) takes on both of these topics, while Coleman's seminal *Business and Politics: A Study of Collective Action* (1988) focuses on the methods firms use in lobbying. My study builds on these foundations by zeroing in on the development of the policy instrument preferences of business.

Questions of how much influence business has on public policy outcomes in Canada are, as such, beyond the scope of this particular inquiry. Such questions require a fundamentally different research design than those related to how business creates the preferences for which it ultimately attempts to exert influence. Indeed, before one can undertake a systematic study of business influence on public policy in Canada, one first needs to know how those preferences were developed.

A unique contribution of this work, however, is its demonstration of how politics influences business preferences for policy instruments relating to climate change. Not only does the current political context feed into expectations about regulatory stability, but previous government choices affect firms' preferences by providing some firms with experience with particular instruments. Thus, business preferences are not exogenous, but endogenous, to the business-government relationship. Although themes related to the effect of political institutions on business policy preferences can be found in some of the political economy literature, this book's explanation of the mechanism by which politics matters – by affecting expectations and, therefore, perceptions of risk and advantage – is novel.

Omitted but not Forgotten

The reader might notice that I do not spend much time discussing environmental advocacy groups and their effect on business actions or preferences. Many might find this surprising, particularly given that much research in the United States has examined the power of lobby groups, of which environmental non-governmental organizations (ENGOs) are a subset, in relation to policy-making in that country. Although my research design was not developed to investigate non-governmental influence on public policy, I found no corresponding influence on business policy instrument preferences in the Canadian case. Indeed, it was not so much that the representatives of firms and associations I interviewed argued against the influence of ENGOs as that they completely neglected to think of them, unless directly prompted – in which case, they responded overwhelmingly that the influence of ENGOs was not a significant factor in their choice of preference. Instead, when asked if they felt pressure from any groups, they talked about their shareholders, their investors, and their customers. This is not to say that environmental groups have had no influence on firms' environmental actions but there is no evidence thus far that environmental groups have played a significant role in determining firms' choice of climate policy instruments. The sole exception is the forestry industry, where major protests by ENGOs against clear-cut logging in the 1990s were a major catalyst for that industry's progressive stand on environmental issues. However, as I discuss in detail in Chapter 6, the forestry industry also had a considerable advantage over other industries when it came to climate change policy instruments, particularly cap-and-trade. Having access to a technically zero-emitting fuel source at little cost in the form of waste biomass, the industry could expect to make money in a carbon-trading market.

The general lack of perceived influence of environmental groups on firms' public policy instrument preferences would not be surprising, however, to many observers of Canadian parliamentary government. Canada's Westminster-style political system – where power is centralized in the Prime Minister's Office (PMO) and in cabinet (Savoie 2003) – differs greatly from that of the United States. As such, it is challenging for environmental organizations to influence policy outcomes at the federal level without the support of the prime minister and the prime minister's entourage. Moreover, Canada's environmental laws, written, of course, by the very governments whose power is enhanced by centralized control, do not provide for the same litigious pathways for grievance as do US environmental laws. Only when environmental groups are able to mobilize public opinion significantly – as in the case of the protests against the forestry industry in the 1990s – can they force governments and/or industry to act. If ENGOs have little power in the policy process in Canada, firms are unlikely to pay attention to their concerns in establishing preferences for policy instrument, as this study finds.[3]

Outline of the Book

This book summarizes an exercise in model building. The first two chapters discuss the foundations of the risk-advantage model and how it was developed. Chapter 2 briefly summarizes the most pertinent scholarly literature on the subject and how it laid the foundation for this research. Chapter 3 then examines in detail the methods I used and their basis in the political science literature. In the remaining chapters, I examine the evidence – in addition to the interview data from which it was developed – supporting and, in one case, contradicting the model as developed. Chapter 4 employs process-tracing methodology to demonstrate that public attentiveness to climate change policy instruments correlated with a major shift in business preferences. Chapter 5 examines the link between public opinion and investors' concerns, which the model suggests should be related. Chapter 6 examines the significance of advantage, and Chapter 7 looks at the significance of experience.

As much as possible, I have attempted to create falsifiable tests of the model, and in Chapter 8 I present a null finding from one of these exercises: that there is little evidence to suggest that, independent of

---

3 The observant reader might have noted that no one from the PMO was interviewed for this study. At the time of research, access to the Stephen Harper PMO and to all political staffers was highly constrained by government policies controlling communications. Neither scholars nor journalists were given access to high-level officials in the Harper government, a chilling of discussion between the government and outsiders, including researchers, that limited the available interview subjects. Since the topic here is business preferences for government policy instruments, not business influence on government policy, I do not believe this limitation undermines the study in any significant way. Additionally, as I discuss in Chapter 4, we have a very good understanding, from both ministerial staff and business officials, of the relationship between the Liberal government and business (particularly the petroleum sector) prior to the Conservatives' coming to power in 2006. I suspect, however, that only now, with a new Liberal government in power, might we be able to learn whether this relationship changed substantially during Mr Harper's period in office. Until then, we will have to take business's word on its side of the equation and that of the government officials who were available for interview. Chapter 4 relays what is known now.

previous experience, managers' ideas influenced preferences. I incorporated the ideas variable into the initial incarnation of the model, but dropped it in the discussion due to this lack of evidence. Managers' ideas about risk still might influence business action on the environment, however – a possibility I discuss in Chapter 8.

I conclude, in Chapter 9, with a discussion of the implications of my findings for future research. Ultimately, the goal of this book is to present evidence that the risk-advantage model accounts for business preferences for climate change policy instruments in Canada in a much more nuanced way than any other known explanation.

Chapter Two

A Literary Foundation

In the wide literature on business-government relations and firms' decision-making, perceptions of firms' preferences for government policy instruments fall into two paradigmatic categories: the "cost-benefit" paradigm and the "relational" paradigm. In the former, firms' preferences are seen as resulting from a rational calculation of cost and benefit. Although some authors see this as a simple calculation of the cost to the firm of an instrument, others argue that government policy and policy instruments actually can entail benefits by affecting a firm's competitive position in the marketplace. In the latter, firms' preferences are perceived as dependent on relationships, either between the firm and other actors (external pressure and coordination problems) or between managers within the firm (internal politics and/or ideas of managers). Each paradigm has something to tell us about the case of business preferences for climate change policy instruments in Canada, although neither gives us the whole picture. They are, nonetheless, the foundation of the risk-advantage model, which also provides a framework for understanding how the multiple explanatory variables discussed in the literature work together in determining business preferences for climate change policy instruments.

Costs and Benefits

A common current in the environmental policy literature in Canada and the United States is that environmental policy is developed in opposition to business interests and influence. Business is perceived as inhabiting one side of an adversarial policy divide, in opposition to environmental groups and other proponents (Ackerman 1985; Harrison 1996a; Litfin 2000; VanNijnatten 1999). There is strong logic in favour of this perspective: environmental regulations by their nature create cost burdens for polluters – overwhelmingly heavy industry – and, consequently, industry can be expected to fight this imposition, unless the policy provides clear financial gain, as with particular contracts or subsidies (Harrison 1996a; Kincaid 1996; Litfin 2000). Indeed, from this perspective, authors note that it is somewhat puzzling why we have environmental regulations at all, given the strength of industry versus environmental groups (Harrison 1996a). Government can be expected to avoid "alienating" job-creating industry, and thus avoid creating stringent environmental regulations, but this pattern can be overcome in times of high public salience of the issue or through participatory governance models, which limit the strength of the industrial lobby (Harrison 1996a; Rabe 1999; VanNijnatten 1999).

The assumption, either explicit or implicit, in this significant literature is that business's interest where environmental policy is concerned is equivalent to cost avoidance, particularly because most environmental policies cannot be expected to provide direct financial gains to most sectors or firms. Harrison sums up this perspective:

> Regulation can be broadly defined as rules of behaviour backed by the legitimate sanctions of the state. In effect rather than providing a public service itself, either directly or indirectly, the government exercises its coercive powers to force someone else to provide the service and to pay for it. Thus, an important characteristic of regulation is that the costs borne by government to administer the program tend to be small relative to the costs borne by the private sector.
>
> Regulation typically is perceived as imposing concentrated costs on regulated industries in order to confer diffuse benefits on the public. One would not expect governments to pursue such regulatory policies aggressively, since those affected by diffuse benefits generally would be uninformed, unorganized and thus unappreciative, while regulated interests would be well organized and unyielding in their opposition. (Harrison 1996a, 13)

It is from this perspective that the support of the Canadian Association of Petroleum Producers and the Canadian Council of Chief Executives for carbon pricing appears the most puzzling. If limiting compliance costs were the main goal of business in interacting with government on environmental policy, why would Canadian industrial groups lobby for a carbon price over subsidies or voluntary agreements?

One possible answer to this question is that they really are not offer-ing any such support. The term "greenwash" gained currency when Greenpeace published a booklet by Kenny Bruno entitled "The Green-peace Book of Greenwash" at the 1992 Earth Summit in Rio de Janeiro. Bruno defined "greenwash" as the phenomenon by which "transna-tional corporations are preserving and expanding their market share by posing as friends of the environment and leaders in the struggle to eradicate poverty" (Bruno 1992, 1). A number of books about corporate manipulation of the environmental agenda were later published, many arguing that large corporations hide environmental destruction behind green public relations (Ehrlich and Ehrlich 1996; Greer and Bruno 1998; Rowell 1996). Translated to this case, this perspective would suggest that firms are claiming to support carbon pricing when in reality they are working behind the scenes to prevent its implementation. For these authors, large business and environmental policy cannot walk hand in hand.

Others, however, disagree that environmental policy is always bad for business and that firms that support such policies must be lying. Business success, they argue, is a complex exercise, and might involve taking on greater cost to gain a competitive advantage in the mar-ket. Porter and van der Linde, for example, suggest that "[p]roperly designed environmental standards can trigger innovation, which may partially or totally offset the cost of complying with them. Such innova-tion offsets, as we call them, can not only lower the net costs of meeting environmental standards but can even lead to absolute advantages for firms in foreign countries not subject to them" (1995, 98). This might lead firms to prefer and even lobby for more stringent environmental standards.

As a case in point, Garcia-Johnson (2000) found that US companies operating in Mexico actually pushed for more stringent environmental regulation in order to create a competitive advantage over domestic Mexican corporations. As they had already adapted to more stringent regulation in the United States, it was less costly for them to continue those practices in Mexico and more costly for Mexican competitors that had not yet adopted higher standards. Vogel (1995) found a similar pat-tern in relation to environmental regulation between states. Far from supporting a race to the bottom, therefore, firms are actually advocat-ing a race to the top.

Along a similar vein, but in a different policy area, the litera-ture on firm and country preferences for protectionism versus trade liberalization implies that the cost-benefit analysis of a government policy option is complex and dependent on particular market factors. Arguments generally fall into one of three categories (see Kingstone 1999): that preferences for or against liberalization are a function of (i) the profile of production – whether a firm is export oriented or domestic dependent (Gourovitch 1977; Milner and Yoffie 1989); or (ii) the abundance and scarcity of an industry's resources (land, labour, or capital) – if resources are scarce, the firm or industry prefers protection, if resources are abundant, it prefers trade (Rogowski 1987); or (iii) the mobility of factors – if a firm or industry can move easily, it prefers trade (Frieden 1991). This literature, which is one of the few that focuses exclusively on the development of firms' policy preferences, highlights the fact that government policy affects firms differently depending on the industry's characteristics: some firms might gain, while others lose. Preferences cannot, therefore, be assumed based on the policy instrument, but require an in-depth analysis of the industry.

What all these arguments have in common is a belief that firms' preferences are based on an analysis of the costs and benefits of a policy instrument. If an instrument entails significant costs, a firm could still support it if it was likely to provide significant benefit, usually involving increasing market share, creating a competitive advantage over other firms, or providing a rationale for innovation.

Along these same lines, a firm might also support a policy instrument if it is considered the least costly of a bad lot. One could argue that firms support particular types of carbon pricing because they believe it is inevitable, and want to influence the type of price chosen to ensure the cheapest option – say, a grandfathered cap-and-trade program over a carbon tax. This is a mixture of the simple cost and greenwash arguments, since it suggests that firms do not actually support carbon pricing, but merely want to get the best deal available. A firm's preferences, therefore, would be based on expectations of future government strategy implementation and a simple analysis of cost.

Within the cost-benefit analysis paradigm, therefore, there are three potential explanations for the perceived variation in business preferences for climate change policy instruments. Although simple cost of compliance clearly does not explain the case, greenwash, competitive strategy (based on different market factors and the characteristics of the industry), and expectations for future government policy (getting the cheapest of a bad lot) could all conceivably explain the puzzle.

Relational Paradigm

Not all authors agree, however, that preferences are based on analyses of the costs and benefits of the policy instrument. Some argue that relationships, either between the firm and other actors or among managers within the firm, have a significant impact on preferences. Henriques and Sadorsky (2008) examine the determinants of firm engagement with unilateral voluntary environmental agreements such as Responsible Care, where there is no direct government involvement. They find that both forestalling future regulatory implementation *and* maintaining public trust through improved environmental performance and better stakeholder relations (with customers, investors, and the community) were key reasons firms might create voluntary agreements among themselves. Although these agreements are independent of government action and, therefore, analytically different than the policy instruments discussed here, this work, along with other studies in the corporate social responsibilities literature (Gunningham 2009), provides further evidence of the significance of stakeholders for firm action on the environment.

On the specific topic of business preferences for government policy instruments, Doug Macdonald's field-defining 2007 book, *Business and Environmental Politics in Canada,* makes a similar argument. In a review of four decades of environmental politics in Canada, Macdonald develops a theoretical explanation of firms' actions with respect to environmental policy. His goals are ambitious: he examines the objectives of businesses, their political strategies and tactics, and the source and extent of their power. He argues that the traditional profit motive, either cost minimization or revenue extraction, is not the only objective of firms' interaction with government; the need for legitimacy is a distinct second objective. Moreover, Macdonald contends that firms' responses to regulation are determined more by the degree of threat posed by the regulation – in particular, the coerciveness of the instrument and the impact of the issue – than by corporate culture. Success in meeting these objectives, Macdonald argues, is linked to external factors, including the institutional context, government motivations and public opinion, and the prevailing view of the relationship between state and society – for example, large government versus small government.

Macdonald's work provides one possible answer to the research question in this study: the search for legitimacy might cause firms to change their preference for public policy instruments in response to public opinion. In this regard, however, his findings are extremely useful but inconclusive, largely because of questions related to the concept of legitimacy. For one, Macdonald leaves "legitimacy" undefined, creating confusion over what he is actually arguing. Nonetheless, assuming that legitimacy refers to public support for the firm and its practices, it remains unclear why it matters to firms. Although Macdonald states that "legitimacy is necessary for basic survival" and is part of "a longer-term strategy for achieving profits," he goes on to argue that "legitimacy is not just a secondary interest, contributing to the primary political goal of profit. It is instead a distinct and separate interest" (Macdonald 2007, 31). This contradiction is never explained. What is clear is that, for Macdonald, firms' preferences are developed in relation to public opinion. What is unclear is why firms care about their public image, and how that motivation is related to other possible motivations, such as profitability and the long-term survival of the firm. In other words, although MacDonald's work suggests a relational argument, it could merely be a new expression of the cost-benefit paradigm discussed above.

Another group of scholars provides an alternative explanation: that firms care about their relationships with other actors, conceivably, although not explicitly, including the public, because the relationships themselves are important for business success. In their book and subsequent work, Hall and Soskice (2003) along with numerous colleagues develop an analytical framework using "comparative institutional advantage," a concept based on the premise that a nation's political institutions influence the strategies of its firms and lead to economies that are advantaged in certain types of production over others. The authors perceive "firms as actors seeking to develop and exploit core competencies or dynamic capabilities understood as capacities for developing, producing, and distributing goods and services profitably." Success in these ventures, however, is dependent on others and, therefore, on the firm's "ability to coordinate effectively with a wide range of actors" (Hall and Soskice 2003, 6). But this coordination is problematic given the firm's lack of control over other actors, so firms turn to political institutions to help mitigate or eliminate such problems.

Hall and Soskice's framework highlights five "spheres" in which firms might face coordination problems: industrial relations (bargaining with unions over wages), vocational training and education, corporate governance (investors), interfirm relations, and employees. Ultimately, the authors argue that firms will support political institutions that resolve their coordination problems. They seek institutions that reduce uncertainty in their relationships with others and allow them and others to make credible commitments to one another.[4]

In addition to providing a unique and explicit conceptualization of the firm as a political actor, Hall and Soskice also highlight the fact that different institutional dynamics in different countries can be expected to have different effects on firms' actions. They argue that the "availability of different modes of coordination conditions the efficiency with which firms perform certain activities" (2003, 38). They differentiate between liberal market economies (LMEs), such as Canada, the United States, the United Kingdom, Australia, and New Zealand, and coordinated market economies (CMEs) such as Germany, Japan, Switzerland, the Netherlands, and Sweden. Firms in LMEs rely largely on markets to deal with coordination problems, while firms in CMEs generally rely on non-market coordination and, often, formalized strategic interaction among actors.

Of particular relevance to the Canadian case and to Macdonald's argument about public opinion is that investors in LMEs are forced by law to rely on public information about companies in making their investment decisions. This makes them fickle and flighty, and more likely to bolt at the first sign of risk. Investors in LMEs are also more interested in short-term gains, which are seen as the main indicator of the health of the corporation. In CMEs, on the other hand, institutions created to ensure the involvement of investors, employees, and other stakeholders within firms' decision-making bodies ensure that investors have more inside information about firms' activities than do investors in LMEs and, consequently, are able to focus on long-term growth even in the face of short-term losses. Canadian managers, therefore, would be expected to be far more preoccupied by investors' concerns than are firms in CMEs such as Germany; moreover, in Canada, investors' impressions are based on the firm's public image, and so the firm must also be concerned about its reputation and legitimacy.

Interactions between the firm and other actors, whether government, investors, or the public, are not the only relationships deemed in the literature to be important to business preferences. In a study of voluntary environmental program adoption by two US companies, Prakash

---

4 Hall and Soskice define institutions as "a set of rules, formal or informal, that actors generally follow, whether for normative, cognitive, or material reasons" (2003, 9).

(2000) argues that leadership and power dynamics between key managers affect a firm's willingness to adopt programs that offer no clear profit motivation. Explicitly contrary to the cost-benefit paradigm, this view contends that one cannot assume that firms will avoid environmental programs that increase costs while providing no revenue.

Other work in economics and sociology supports this perspective. In particular, Cyert and March's *A Behavioral Theory of the Firm* (1993) describes the firm as made up of a "coalition of multiple, conflicting interests" whose goals are determined by the "dominant coalition" within the firm. Thus, reminiscent of liberal perspectives in international relations, in this view firms are defined by the preferences of a subgroup of individuals within the organization, not by any natural tendency. As power flows to certain individuals over others, preferences will change. The limitation of this argument is that it does not explain why individuals hold the preferences they do. The focus on individual managers' preferences in determining firms' preferences, however, can be perceived as highlighting the significance of the ideas of key managers in preference development. For example, Gunningham (2009), in arguing that firms are attempting to meet their "license to operate" when creating corporate environmental programs, suggests that managers' perceptions of environmental and social demands by stakeholders, as well as the threats versus the opportunities of acting, influence the level of environmental action they take. Although the psychology literature on individual decision-making might explain individuals' perceptions and, from a relational perspective, firms' preferences, it is sufficient at this juncture – and follows a recent trend in political science – to say that the ideas of key decision-makers could influence firms' preferences for climate change policy instruments significantly.

Taken together, therefore, the literature provides five hypotheses about business preferences for climate change policy instruments in addition to the traditional cost avoidance argument:

1) *greenwash:* firms lie about their support for carbon pricing in order to increase their market share or improve their reputation;
2) *competitive advantage and market factors:* competitive strategies based on market factors and the characteristics of the industry lead firms to support carbon pricing;
3) *expectations:* expectations of future government policy implementation (that carbon pricing is inevitable) lead firms to support a particular carbon-pricing instrument;

4) *external pressure:* pressure from, or coordination problems with, external actors, particularly government, the public, and investors, leads firms to support carbon pricing; and
5) *ideas:* the ideas of managers belonging to the dominant group in the firm determine preferences.

As is traditional in this discipline, these hypotheses provided the foundation for my fieldwork and the initial research design. As I sat across from executives at business associations in Ottawa, Montreal, Calgary, and Vancouver in 2009, it was not long before it became clear that these hypotheses and the variables inherent in them were wholly insufficient and could not, on their own, provide the key to understanding the puzzle. It was not that none was important – interview subjects referred to components of several (which I discuss in greater detail in Chapter 3) – but how they related to one another and under what conditions certain variables were significant while others were not remained unclear. Something was missing. Getting at that something required a re-examination of my question and the creation of a new model. This, in turn, required an adaptation of my methodology. It is to this exercise in model-building and the methods behind it that I now turn.

Chapter Three

Methods for Model-building

The support of the Canadian Association of Petroleum Producers (CAPP) and the Canadian Council of Chief Executives (CCCE) for carbon pricing in 2008 highlighted a significant puzzle. Unfortunately, unravelling this puzzle was not a straightforward exercise and, in the end, a three-phase research project was required. In the first phase, I developed a traditional structured, focused comparative methodology and undertook interviews. A preliminary analysis of the interview data, however, revealed weaknesses in the initial hypotheses, which led to a second phase of model-building based on a previously overlooked variable: risk. The third phase involved the development of testable propositions based on the model and the collection of new data to determine if the model was indeed relevant in this case. I report the findings of this final phase in subsequent chapters. Here, I lay out the methodological process and problems inherent in each phase, highlighting the foundations of the research design within the methodological literature.

Phase 1: Initial Research Design and Fieldwork

Initially, I interpreted the puzzle as follows: despite the lower costs to the firm of voluntary agreements and subsidies, there was variation in business preference across the spectrum of possible policy instruments. At the time, no survey of current business preferences for climate change policy instruments was available, but as I thought it unlikely that all firms and associations would support a costlier policy instrument, I assumed that the position of the CCCE and CAPP represented one of many within the wider business community. I therefore stated my initial research question as: *What causes variation in business prefer-ences for climate change policy instruments in Canada?*

Armed with the five hypotheses detailed in Chapter 2 (greenwash, competitive advantage and market factors, expectations, external pres-sure, and ideas), I developed a comparative research design (see George and Bennett 2005; King, Keohane, and Verba 1994) to test the signifi-cance of each hypothesis. I anticipated that, in comparing preferences of different business groups in relation to the variables inherent in the hypotheses, it would be possible to determine the significance of each hypothesis. To increase the number of observations, I included both associations and firms in the research design, defining participants' characteristics to ensure appropriate comparison.

On the association side, I opened the study to all national associa-tions of large, final-emitting sectors, representing large corporations, to ensure that all participating sectors would be regulated under all pol-icy instruments. Since most cap-and-trade programs formally regulate only large final emitters, the inclusion of sectors, such as services, that are not directly affected by a particular instrument could have caused substantial bias in the data. The only exception was the auto industry – represented by the Canadian Motor Vehicle Association – whose opera-tions are not strictly heavy emitting, but which has played a historic role in Canadian climate change policy debates, particularly around the issue of tailpipe standards.

The inclusion of associations primarily representing large corpo-rations was necessary because the decision-making process within such large firms was expected to be substantially different from that of small businesses. Certainly it appeared inappropriate to compare AbitibiBowater, for example, with a mom-and-pop flower shop. Con-sequently, among Canada's multisectoral business associations, I included only the CCCE, as the others (such as the Canadian Cham-ber of Commerce and Canadian Manufacturers & Exporters) represent both large and small business alike.

The firms included in the study were limited to three industry "cases" – cement, oil and gas, and forestry[5] – chosen to provide variation

---

5 Interestingly, due to the realities of each of these sectors, the participating firms were overwhelmingly publicly traded companies, rather than privately held firms. This had the positive effect of ensuring that all participating firms faced similar pressure from shareholders, but it also prevented a comparative analysis of this influence, as no control group of private firms was present.

on the cost of compliance, the traditional explanatory variable, since each industry would face a different cost effect from regulatory instruments such as cap-and-trade and carbon taxation. At one end of the spectrum, the forestry industry could be expected to pay very little under any carbon-pricing policy instrument due to the availability of a free – in the sense that a firm would not need to purchase it from another firm – and technically zero-emitting fuel source in waste biomass. Indeed, with respect to cap-and-trade, the forestry industry could be expected to gain revenue from the sale of allowances to other industries should it update its boilers from oil or natural gas to biomass.

At the other end of the spectrum, the cement industry could face substantial and possibly fatal cost increases from carbon pricing. Approximately 50 per cent of emissions from cement production in North America is the result of fixed processes – emissions created through the chemical process of making cement. Unlike fuel-related emissions, no available technology, such as fuel-switching, allows for a decrease in these emissions. Moreover, cement production is highly emissions intensive: 1.0 tonne of cement produces approximately 0.89 of a tonne of carbon dioxide (Hendriks et al. 2004). If a price on carbon were placed on all emissions, even one as low as $10 per tonne, it could be expected to decrease profitability in the cement industry substantially. For example, if cement sold for $100 per tonne, $9 of that – or 9 per cent of the return – could go to tax. If profits were 15 per cent, or $15 per tonne of cement, profitability would decrease by half; if the carbon price were $20 per tonne, there would be no profit at all in this scenario.

In between these two extremes, the oil and gas sector would not face equivalent process emissions. It also has lower emissions intensity, even in the high-emitting oil sands, where, as of 2008, 0.6 of a tonne of carbon dioxide was emitted per tonne of oil produced (Droitsch, Huot, and Partington 2010).[6] Moreover, the oil and gas industry makes much higher profits per tonne of CO_2 than does the cement industry and, without fixed-process emissions, has much more capacity to decrease emissions.

Early on in the research, it became clear that petroleum producers face a very different set of incentives with respect to climate change policy instruments than do natural gas producers, because natural gas

---

6 The conversion from barrels of oil is as follows: 7.2 barrels of oil is equivalent to 1 tonne of oil; 83 kilograms of CO_2 per barrel of oil is equivalent to 597.6 kilograms (0.597 of a tonne) of CO_2 per tonne of oil.

is far less emissions intensive (when consumed) than oil. Consequently, natural gas firms could be advantaged by climate change policy instruments targeted mainly at oil or coal, and it would be inappropriate for me to analyse the two types of fossil fuels as one. Accordingly, I separated them into two "cases," and sent more natural gas producers invitations to participate. To corroborate the claims of business actors and to test the significance of the greenwash hypothesis, I also included twenty-two "elite observers" of business policy instrument preferences, including government officials with whom industry regularly negotiates, observers from non-governmental organizations (NGOs), and consultants.

From late 2008 to August 2009, fieldwork in Ottawa, Vancouver, Calgary, and Montreal resulted in sixty interviews with business executives and elite observers. In total, seventeen firms and thirteen associations participated. The interview subject was generally the organization's chief executive officer (CEO) or director of the environment; in some cases, more than one official from a firm or association participated (the choice was that of the firm or association). Associations from all known heavy-emissions sectors participated (see the Appendix for the list of interviews). The goal was to include five firms from each of the petroleum, forestry, natural gas, and cement sectors; in the end, five firms participated from the petroleum and forestry sectors, three from the natural gas sector, and four from the cement sector. I also included evidence from TransAlta, an Alberta electrical utility, because the chair of the National Round Table on the Environment and the Economy, Robert Page, had been a senior executive at that firm for ten years, and much of his testimony related to it. I have not included TransAlta as a "participating firm," however, because Page was not an official at the firm at the time of his testimony. The data from Transalta, therefore, is supplementary to the overall comparative design.

Phase 2: Model-building

During the preliminary phase, subject testimonials pointed to two unexpected findings that highlighted challenges with the research design. First, instead of variation in business preferences across the spectrum of climate change policy instruments, all but three firms and associations articulated support for a price on carbon, although they differed on the type of carbon price – cap-and-trade or carbon taxation – they preferred. Interviewees referred to a shift in the business community towards support for carbon pricing that had occurred about three years earlier. Thus, where I expected variation, instead preferences were clustered at one end of the spectrum of possible policy instrument choices. This suggested that the firms and associations participating in the study might not be as independent as I first thought, a common pitfall of case study research (George and Bennett 2005). Indeed, some interviewees testified that other groups and associations – particularly the CCCE and the Industry Steering Committee on Climate Change, a group created in the late 1990s to ensure a common industry voice – had influenced their firm's or association's choice.

This new empirical evidence led to a conceptual shift in my understanding of the puzzle. Two interdependent questions now required answers. First, why had almost the entire business community shifted its preference to support carbon pricing? Second, why did support for the type of carbon price, either cap-and-trade or carbon taxation, vary? In other words, what caused variation in business preferences for climate change policy instruments over time and among organizations? Although a comparative research design conceivably could "get at" the second question, the first question suggested that this might not be a multicase study after all, but a single-case study with a clear temporal element. As such, a method such as process-tracing might be more useful in exploring the issue. Moreover, it was clear that the interview data alone would be insufficient for understanding the case.

Second, the initial elaboration of the hypotheses, while demonstrating some value, also presented a challenge in that they did not completely explain the empirical findings. Although subject testimony suggested some support for four out of the five hypotheses, none stood out among the group. In particular, some subjects pointed to competitive advantage as significant (particularly in the forestry and natural gas sectors); others suggested that ideational factors such as the convictions and beliefs of their CEO or familiarity with a previous policy instrument played a role. Interviewees made little reference to pressure from environmental NGOs, employees, or unions, but that from investors and shareholders were of considerable concern. Finally, some respondents referred to government moves in Alberta, British Columbia, and at the federal level towards regulation in 2007 and 2008 in explaining their preference choices; this suggests that their expectations of government policy implementation also might have been significant. Why expectations mattered was unclear, however:

if firms were merely choosing the least costly among *probable* policy instruments, as the hypothesis assumed, why did some now support taxation (the most costly policy instrument) and others have no official preference for the type of carbon price? Should they not now all support grandfathered cap-and-trade? Nonetheless, only the greenwash hypothesis had no support, as government officials testified that sector representatives were saying the same thing behind closed doors as in public.

The problem was that, at this stage, there was no clear winner among the hypotheses and no clear link or framework for understanding how they related to one another. Although multiple factors might have been at play, a new variable came to light during the research that appeared to convey a mental model that might tie the hypotheses together. That variable was risk. Encana's executive advisor and former vice president Gerry Protti had this to say:

> We categorize our risks on a wide range of issues, extremely wide and we have a chief risk officer in our corporation ... When you look at climate, that has both materiality [and reputational] issues depending upon the type of regulation you're talking about. If it's extremely ill defined and we've announced we're going to produce 400,000 barrels of heavy oil out of northeastern Alberta over the next 15 years – which we have announced – and, well, your investors say, what happens [if ...]? What could happen under current emissions policies? Well, you then develop scenarios and the less well defined the legislative, regulative and the political environment is, the more risk there is.

From Suncor Energy's vice president of sustainable development, Gordon Lambert:

> It's unacceptable to have a policy void ... [W]e as a sector, because we're oil producers, we end up holding the lightning rod for the debate and it really is governments that need to step up and declare public interest. Because even as companies we are not a proxy for the public interest. But we are having to make long term investment decisions and so you do need certainty in declaring the public interest in order to do what we do. So if we are always in this perpetual state of anxiety ... [For instance, the government says] wait until next year comes around. It really is difficult. We don't know what to convey to investors. They don't know how to assess the risk.

And from the Canadian Gas Association's president Michael Cleland:

> You are shifting along a sort of risk spectrum, no question about that. And the risk of not acting is starting to show up with, you know, you have your shareholders, you have insurance companies, you have all sorts of people who worry about securities and various types of things who say, "what are you doing to deal with your carbon intensity?" You've got, frankly, a public image, brand risk. And those start to accumulate at the other end and start to over balance the risk that you're going to incur a bunch of costs that you might have preferred to avoid. Or that your business model is going to disappear out from underneath you. Or that you are going to go and make a bunch of investments that are going to turn out to have been completely stupid. And that's always there as a possibility but it's [immense now] as compared to ten years ago.

It is not unusual for case studies to bring attention to a previously overlooked variable; indeed, it is one of the main strengths of case study methodology. According to George and Bennett (2005, 20):

> Case studies have powerful advantages in the heuristic identification of new variables and hypotheses through the study of deviant or outlier cases and in the course of field work – such as archival research and interviews with participants, area experts, and historians. When a case study researcher asks a participant "were you thinking X when you did Y" and gets the answer, "No, I was thinking Z," then if the researcher had not thought of Z as a causally relevant variable, she may have a new variable demanding to be heard.

George and Bennett describe the situation I faced when interview subjects, too often to be coincidence, discussed their policy instrument preferences in terms of "risk." It remained unclear, however, what business executives meant exactly when using the term in referring to climate change policy instruments and how it related to the initial hypotheses.

A point of methodological clarity is required here. Although the significance of the concept of risk began to become apparent about halfway through the interview process, I did not change the questions I asked subjects so as to examine specifically the relationship between risk and preferences of climate change policy instrument. Doing so might have added to the data related to the topic, it also might have introduced confirmation bias into those data. Accordingly, the only change I made was to ask subjects what they meant by risk, if the topic came up without prompting, in an attempt to zero in on a definition.

Risk is such a commonplace term in the business lexicon that, when asked to clarify, subjects often had trouble doing so, and generally provided only a circular definition that used the term risk to define risk. The next phase of the research, therefore, involved an analysis of business professional texts on risk management and business administration more generally to "get at" the concept of risk and to determine the implications of the pervasive use of the concept in setting preferences. This was guided by three questions: What is "risk" in this context? Why does it matter? What does it imply for our understanding of business preferences for climate change policy instruments?

As discussed in Chapter 1, despite numerous possible definitions of risk, the investment management definition appeared to best fit the manner in which subjects widely used the term – namely, risk is uncertainty that an investment will receive the expected return. Indeed, during this stage, it became clear that risk and the associated implication of investor concern could help explain the relationships among the advantage, ideas, expectations, and pressure group (significance of investors, in this case) hypotheses. Risk was the key to explaining the puzzle.

The first part of the model as initially developed was the same as the final version described in Chapter 1. In determining preferences for climate change policy instruments, managers seek to:

1) limit the risk of the policy instrument to *capital investments*;
2) limit the effects of the policy instrument on the risk perceptions of *external investors*; and
3) seek *advantage* where possible.

At this stage, however, the second part of the model varied slightly from the final version in Chapter 1. It was clear that the requirement to limit risk to capital investment *while* assuaging investors' concerns *and* seeking advantage was no simple feat, particularly given uncertainty about instrument design and the likelihood of implementation. The second part of the model, therefore, states that, where there is ambiguity about the weighting of risk and advantage, managers turn to other ideational factors to fill the gaps. Interview subjects suggested that business executives look to their own experience or to the convictions and beliefs of leaders to fill knowledge gaps and add to certainty about the effects of a particular policy instrument. As I discuss below, I left the connection between ideas and expectations implicit at this stage.

Initially, I based the model on the superficial results of the interview process (deeming that what interview subjects stated was important). Despite its inclusion in previous hypotheses, therefore, I did not include corporate culture in the model because interviewees did not widely consider it important; rather, they largely argued that culture could be reduced to the convictions and beliefs of the CEO. Equally, interviewees overwhelming ignored pressure groups such as ENGOs, and the interview data contained no evidence that such groups had any impact on firms' preferences. Interviewees often mentioned investors and shareholders, however, and these groups consequently became central to the model.

As stated above, the most noteworthy contribution of the risk variable to this study is its ability to provide a structure and explanation for the varied significance of the initial hypotheses. Competitive advantage, ideas, and investors (pressure groups) are included directly in the model: if a public policy instrument offers an advantage, the firm will support it. If no advantage exists, the firm must choose between risky options (with respect to both its own investments and those of investors), and where there is ambiguity in weighting, ideational factors come into play.

The significance of expectations, although not explicitly part of the initial model, could also be explained through it, but the explanation varied slightly from the initial articulation based on cost of compliance. In the initial hypothesis, expectations were thought to influence policy instrument preferences because a firm that faced an expectation of policy change would shift preferences to ensure that the cheapest of the *probable* policy options was adopted. The risk-advantage model, however, implies a second possibility: that expectations matter to the firm's policy instrument preferences because they are fundamental to perceptions of risk and advantage. Expectations about future government policy choices affect perceptions of stability in the regulatory context for both the firm and its investors. Once it expects regulatory change, the firm will shift its preference to the most likely policy instrument so as to create stability once again in the regulatory environment and to assuage investors' concerns. Expectations about design details and the impact of those details, based on previous experience with a policy instrument and perceptions of competitive advantage, influence which of the remaining policy instruments the firm will support. Unlike under the initial expectations hypothesis, therefore, the firm will not necessarily support the least costly of the remaining policy instruments. If the firm perceives a competitive advantage in an instrument and/or has experience with a particular instrument, it is likely to support that instrument. Experience appears to trump advantage in this analysis, a finding I discuss in detail in Chapters 6 and 7.

Phase 3: Proposition-testing

George and Bennett contend that

> [a]n inductively derived explanation of a case can also involve more novel theories and variables. In this context, researchers are frequently advised not to develop a theory from evidence and then test it against the same evidence; facts cannot test or contradict a theory that is constructed around them. In addition, using the same evidence to create and test a theory also exacerbates risks of confirmation bias, a cognitive bias toward affirming one's own theories that has been well documented both in laboratory experiments and in the practices of social scientists.
>
> However, it is valid to develop a theory from a case and then test the theory against additional evidence from the case that was not used to derive the theory. This makes the theory falsifiable as an explanation for the case, and can circumvent confirmation bias ... Indeed, in testing a historical explanation of a case, the most convincing procedure is often to develop an explanation from data in the case and then test it against other evidence in the case; otherwise, the only recourse is to test the explanation in other cases that differ in ways that may prevent generalization back to the original case. (George and Bennett 2005, 111–12)

As I stated above, the model I developed was informed both by the testimony of the interview subjects and through a reading of the risk management and business practice literatures. This was not enough, however, to demonstrate its relevance in answering the research question, for two reasons. First, just because interview subjects *claimed* that risk was significant for their policy instrument preferences, this did not mean that concerns about risk management *actually* influenced their policy preference decision-making; for that, one would expect to see particular changes in behaviour that matched expectations. Second, even if risk was indeed important, the model might be an incorrect interpretation of what business executives meant in referring to risk.

Consequently, as George and Bennett argue, a final research phase was required in which I sought new evidence and tested correlations of the observable implications of the model. I then developed five observable implications:

1) the *political context*: since risk is a type of uncertainty, policy instrument preferences should vary with the political context, given that changes in the political context would create uncertainty about the regulatory environment;
2) *public opinion*: investors (like managers) are concerned by the lack of policy certainty and the possible implementation of new policy instruments, but public opinion gives investors (like managers) an indication of possible regulatory change and firms an area of likely investor concern, so firms should respond to public opinion shifts by both shifting preferences *and* changing the way in which they communicate to investors about climate change in their annual reports;
3) *advantage*: firms that perceive an advantage from a policy instrument should support that instrument;
4) *experience*: firms with past experience with a policy instrument should support that instrument; and
5) *convictions and beliefs*: shifts in preferences for climate change policy instruments should follow major changes in personnel at the firm.

In this final phase of the research, I tested each of these observable implications and, therefore, the utility of the model in explaining the case by drawing on new evidence. The evidence I used for this proposition-testing phase included primary source literature from parliamentary committee testimonials, annual reports, government documents, and secondary source material from mass media and scholarly articles. I also used interview data, but only where a clear correlation could be tested and, therefore, falsified – for instance, I compared preferences as articulated in the interviews with previous experience either explained in interviews or determined independently. The only exception relates to the concept of advantage, discussed in Chapter 6; as the significance of competitive advantage for firms is well supported and overwhelmingly accepted in the strategic management literature, I deemed it unnecessary to create a falsifiable test using new data here.

Ultimately, the model-testing phase demonstrated that the risk-advantage model does indeed provide a valid explanation of business preferences for climate change policy instruments in this case. The significance of the convictions and beliefs variable could not, however, be independently verified. At this stage, therefore, I rewrote the model in its final form, both to leave out the convictions and belief variable and to highlight the significance of expectations about future government policy.

Chapter Four

Climate Change Policy Instruments, Business Preferences, and Public Opinion

By shifting our understanding of business motivations from cost-benefit to risk-advantage, we can better understand how different political factors influence business preferences for climate change policy instruments. The political context is significant because changes in that context can create expectations of regulatory change. An expectation of change in the regulatory environment increases the risk to investment, both for the firm itself and for the firm's investors, because the possibility of change makes it challenging to predict the costs associated with regulation over time. In seeking to re-establish regulatory stability and, thus, to decrease investment risk and assuage investors' concerns, firms shift their preferences to expected policy instruments and call for the implementation of those instruments as soon as possible.

In this chapter I test this argument through an exercise of process-tracing: mapping business policy instrument preferences, public opinion, and government policy declarations related to climate change policy instruments from 1988 to 2009. Ultimately, the exercise demonstrates that business preferences for climate change policy instruments began to shift away from voluntary agreements and subsidies towards carbon pricing in late 2006, after public opinion polls began to show that the environment in general and climate change in particular was becoming a top-of-mind issue for Canadians. Prior to 2006, the business community had articulated support only for voluntary agreements, subsidies, or public education, although it did support so-called flexible mechanisms, including emissions-trading systems, during international negotiations (but did not generally support domestic implementation). Thus, the contention of interview subjects that a major shift in business preferences for climate change policy instruments took place in 2006–07 is born out, and a link between that and the political context – particular public attention to the environment – is also supported. I leave to Chapter 4 to explore the question of why that link existed.

To ensure clarity, I separated the historical review into ten distinct periods. At the end of each period, either government policy or business preferences changed, or a major event in climate policy (such as the Kyoto Protocol) took place. As there is considerable literature on government policy on climate change in Canada, this review focuses on business preferences during each period (an area in which the literature is sparse) and provides only a brief summary of government policy in relation to instrument choice (for reviews of government climate policy, see Bernstein 2002; Harrison 2007, 2010; Hoberg and Harrison 1994; Hornung and Bramley 2000; Macdonald 2007; Macdonald and Smith 1999). Moreover, since the review focuses on domestic climate policy and business preferences for domestic policy instruments, I refer to Canada's international treaty negotiations only when they had implications for such preferences. I also highlight changes in public opinion.

The Beginning: 1988–93

Canadian climate change policy was conceived in Toronto at the 1988 World Conference on the Changing Atmosphere, the first major conference on climate change, attended by international scientists and dignitaries, including Prime Minister Brian Mulroney (Bulkeley and Betsill 2003). Over the following five years, the Mulroney government developed policy proposals on climate change and other environmental issues. Many observers, however, criticized the government's 1990 Green Plan as weak and ineffectual, arguing that the plan focused on public education and spending, and avoided any attempt to interfere in business behaviour (Hoberg and Harrison 1994).

Although the media, opposition, and environmental groups were unimpressed by the government's plan, industry and the provinces were far less antagonistic, largely because its weak and vague measures caused little concern (Hoberg and Harrison 1994). Indeed, during the period from 1988 to 1993, business preferences for climate change policy instruments were largely articulated in the negative: business was against regulation of any sort, particularly environmental taxes. When an early draft section of the Green Plan calling for a carbon tax was leaked to the Business Council on National Issues (BCNI, which later became the Canadian Council of Chief Executives, CCCE), the organization reacted swiftly with calls and visits to the Prime Minister's Office (Hoberg and Harrison 1994). Interestingly, the final draft of the plan did not include the offending reference (Morton 1990).

During this period, public attention to environmental issues became significant. From 1988 to 2009 Environics undertook a quarterly poll that asked: "In your opinion, what is the most important problem facing Canadians today?" The polling data provide a good indication of public attention to different issues – particularly the relevant significance of issues in relation to one another and how that changed over time. Over that period, environmental issues went from hardly registering on the poll to being the "most important problem" for a plurality of respondents, suggesting that the environment had become a priority issue for Canadians.

In the poll taken in the third quarter of 1988, environmental issues, then falling under the heading of "pollution," hardly registered among respondents, only 1.1 per cent of whom viewed it as the most important problem. Three months later, 17.6 per cent of respondents cited "pollution" as the most important problem, second only to unemployment among the broad range of problems listed. By the third quarter of 1989, "pollution" was in the top spot, cited as the most important problem by 20.6 per cent of respondents. In 1990 Environics expanded the heading to "pollution/environment," likely in recognition of the significance of broader environmental issues such as climate change. "Pollution/environment" remained the most cited important problem through the third quarter of that year, cited by 16.5 per cent of respondents. In the fourth quarter, however, public attention began to turn away, distracted by economic concerns and the First Gulf War, with only 9.6 per cent of respondents seeing "pollution/environment" as the top problem, a figure that would drop to 2.8 per cent by the fourth quarter of 1992.

Public knowledge about climate change during this period, moreover, was very low. In 1992, 38.6 per cent of Canadians responding to an Environics Environmental Monitor poll believed the phenomenon resulted from the depletion of the ozone layer. Hence, the period from 1989 to 1993 is defined largely by high public attention to environmental issues, low public knowledge of the facts of climate change, and a government that had declared itself unwilling to regulate. Unfortunately, public attention to environmental issues did not reach the heights of the early 1990s again until 2006.

Towards Kyoto: 1993–97

The Chrétien government came into office in 1993 promising to beat the previous government in the environmental policy arena. Initially, however, it allowed civil society to set the pace of action through the Climate Change Task Group, composed of non-governmental organizations (NGOs) and business leaders. The group was set up in response to the instructions of a Joint Ministers' Meeting on 17 November 1994. The Task Group was a multistakeholder forum mandated with "the development of a National Action Program to enable Canada to reach its climate change goals" (Bramley 2000). Co-chaired by Larry Lechner of the Saskatchewan Department of Environment and Sue Kirby of Natural Resources Canada, the group included such diverse interests as Louise Comeau of the Sierra Club and representatives from the Canadian Association of Petroleum Producers.

The Chrétien government hoped the Task Group would achieve consensus on the issue, and had not issued any policy instrument proposals in advance. However, Task Group members complained that the government had provided few resources to the group, leaving them "the impression Ottawa wasn't serious" about the multistakeholder process or the issue (LeBlanc 1995). Many of those involved considered the Task Group a failure, and some environmentalists left the process in frustration in October 1994.

Nonetheless, if the federal government had hoped that the Task Group would provide political cover for future action, it might have been pleased with the outcome. In June 1994, before the environmentalist backlash, the Task Group had published eighty-eight recommendations calling overwhelmingly for the use of voluntary programs, public education, and subsidies, including the suggestion of a voluntary registry and challenge program (Bramley 2000; Hornung and Bramley 2000; Macdonald 2007). The recommendations were injected into the political debate at a time when the Chrétien cabinet was split on the issue. Environment Minister Sheila Copps supported regulation, while Natural Resources Minister Anne McLellan, the government's representative from Alberta, strongly favoured voluntary agreements (Macdonald and Smith 1999). McLellan's view was supported not only by the Task Group, but also by industry more widely: the BCNI, for example, sent out a press release in November entitled "Canada's business leaders outline a voluntary strategy to combat global climate change" (BCNI 1994).

Three months later, it became clear that McLellan had won the battle in cabinet when she signed a Memorandum of Understanding on behalf of her department with the Canadian Association of Petroleum Producers (CAPP). In the Memorandum, the federal government and the oil industry agreed to work together to develop a voluntary carbon registry program (Macdonald and Smith 1999). Then, in February 1995, the government announced its National Action Program on Climate Change, which had as its focal point a Voluntary Challenge Registry, as suggested by the Task Group (Macdonald 2007).

On the international front, both the government and the business community supported "flexible mechanisms" – that is, emissions trading and carbon sinks. In a 1996 speech, BCNI president and CEO Thomas d'Aquino argued that "creative market devices such as emissions trading must be examined to see if such a scheme can bring about results in a lower cost manner" (d'Aquino 1996). He made it clear, however, that he was speaking about international emissions trading; there is no indication that the business community at that time was open to domestic emissions trading or that it would have supported concrete action to implement a Canadian trading system. This makes sense since a global trading system would include all of a firm's competitors in the global market, unlike a domestic trading system, which would include only those firms with headquarters in Canada. Moreover, much of the cost of emissions trading in a global system could be borne by the state if it bought credits from other countries to meet its commitments, consequently, decreasing the impact on domestic producers. Thus, international treaty negotiations aside, the business community, in agreement with government, was strongly in favour of voluntary initiatives from 1993 to 1997. The public remained largely inattentive.

Post-Kyoto: 1997–2001

After the Canadian government agreed under the 1997 Kyoto Protocol to an onerous emissions cut to 6 per cent below 1990 levels, Chrétien tried to mend fences by promising greater consultations with both the provinces and civil society (Harrison 2010). In 1998 the provincial and federal environment and energy ministers jointly initiated a National Climate Change Process. Central to the process was the creation of 16 "issue tables" around which 450 experts from industry, environmental groups, the scientific community and all levels of government would be brought together to discuss climate change policy (Bramley 2000).

The issue tables gave industry representatives an opportunity both to learn about climate change policy instruments and to articulate their preferences. In the report of the Upstream Oil and Gas Working Group, for instance, the oil and gas industry continued to argue in favour of voluntary programs. It conceded that, over the longer term, flexible international mechanisms were reasonable, but it refused to take a stand on domestic emissions trading, going to great lengths to highlight the problems with the policy instrument (CAPP 1999). Thus, throughout the late 1990s, industry remained squarely in favour of voluntary agreements in the near term. In *Action Plan 2000*, which focused on spending programs and public education, the federal government demonstrated its continued accord with industry (Bramley 2000). These programs supplemented the Voluntary Challenge Registry, which remained operational from 1997 to 2004 as a public/private partnership (Macdonald, Houle, and Patterson 2011).

Although aggregate business preference remained decidedly against emissions trading, in 2000 a small number of Canadian companies declared their preference for cap-and-trade. On 17 October seven international companies – three with headquarters in Canada – announced a global initiative with the Washington-based ENGO Environmental DefenseFund, "the primary purpose of [which is] to champion market-based mechanisms" (Environmental Defense Fund 2000). Under this plan, companies would set targets for themselves, which they could meet through reductions or trading. The group, including Canadian companies Alcan, Suncor Energy, and Ontario Hydro, sought to gain real-world experience in emissions trading and push governments to adopt that policy instrument (Environmental Defense Fund 2000).[7] These companies were industry leaders on climate change, and they remind us that, although the business community demonstrated a remarkable uniformity of preference in favour of voluntarism during this time, it was not a homogeneous unit. It is perhaps telling, however, that, of the thousands of companies that could have taken part in such

---

7   Shell International was also a member of the group, but its Canadian affiliate, Shell Canada, was not. At that time, Shell Canada had very different preferences than Shell International. This did not change until 2007, when Shell International bought the remaining shares in the Canadian company and disbanded the Canadian board of directors. I discuss the peculiar relationship between Shell International and Shell Canada in greater detail in Chapter 8.

a global initiative, only seven chose to do so. Cap-and-trade was not in vogue.

The Ratification Debate: 2002

Government climate policy shifted little throughout the 1990s, but in 2002 began a noticeable, if rhetorical, change as the Liberals prepared to ratify the Kyoto Protocol. In May, the federal government published *A Discussion Paper on Canada's Contribution to Addressing Climate Change* (Canada 2002a). The paper laid out three options for Canada's climate change policy: i) a program based on domestic emissions trading; ii) a program based on targeted measures (public information, subsidies, small regulatory changes, and so on); or iii) a mixture of both. With this document, the government signalled for the first time its willingness to move beyond voluntary initiatives and even consider "regulation or, possibly, fiscal measures" in the battle to reduce greenhouse gas emissions.

Meanwhile the conflict between industry and government intensified as, throughout 2002, Canadian corporations and associations mounted their "largest effort to date to influence the environmental policy of the government of Canada," with letters from major associations, particularly CAPP, the CCCE, and the Canadian Chamber of Commerce, sent to the prime minister and relevant ministers (Macdonald 2003).

One of the main targets of industry lobbying was the government's own consultation process. In June 2002 the government held "National Stakeholder Workshops on Climate Change" at locations across the country, in which industry, ENGO, labour, and agriculture representatives could voice their concerns to government and the wider community. The workshops also led industry representatives to realize that several other groups and the federal government did not share their negative perception of ratification (ISC3, 2002).

That same month, the CCCE published a policy statement, "The Kyoto Protocol Revisited: A Responsible and Dynamic Alternative for Canada." The statement succinctly summarized the majority business position on climate change, arguing against regulation with emissions trading because "the various schemes of emissions trading contemplated all would raise costs for Canadian firms beyond those of their major competitors and penalize even highly efficient enterprises" (CCCE 2002, 5). Instead, the statement called for greater public investment in research and development (subsidies) and continued use of voluntary agreements. To support its call for a "Made in Canada" approach, the CCCE continued to dispute the existence of a scientific consensus on climate change. In its policy statement, the organization argued that, "in considering how far to go in imposing real costs on businesses, consumers and taxpayers, Canada must take into account the degree of uncertainty that still surrounds the science of climate change." It went on to quote a well-known sceptic of climate change, Professor Richard Lindzen of the Massachusetts Institute of Technology: "We are not in a position to confidently attribute past climate change to CO_2" (CCCE 2002, 4).

Over the summer of 2002, sensing Mr Chrétien's commitment to the Kyoto Protocol, industry geared up its lobbying efforts. These efforts were purposely organized and industry-wide. In the late 1990s, industry representatives had formed the Industry Steering Committee on Climate Change (known colloquially as ISC3) to allow corporations and industry associations, as an ISC3 official I interviewed put it, "to collaborate, share ideas, and try and create common approaches" on climate change. A 2001 membership list includes the names of thirty business organizations. Most were Ottawa-based business associations, but a few firms – including Imperial Oil, Dow Chemical, and Ontario Power – were also present. By 2002 the ISC3 was playing a central role in coordinating business's response to government climate change policy.

At the group's June 26, 2002 meeting, eighteen associations and firms discussed strategy[8]. Members were encouraged to use multiple forums to lobby Members of Parliament, particularly Liberals. As the meeting minutes record,

> Members agreed that Liberal MPs should be a key part of industry's summer meeting program. It was noted that the Liberal Caucus will hold its summer meeting in Chicoutimi Quebec (August 19-22) and that member

---

8 Present at the meeting were representatives from the Canadian Chemical Producers' Association, the Cement Association of Canada, the Canadian Electricity Association, the Conseil patronal de l'environnement du Québec, the Forest Products Association of Canada, the Canadian Council of Chief Executives, the Canadian Fertilizer Institute, Ontario Power Generation Inc., the Canadian Environment Industry Association, Stelco Inc., the Canadian Energy Pipeline Association, the Canadian Steel Producers Association, the Mining Association of Canada, the Aluminum Association of Canada, the Canadian Chamber of Commerce, Noranda Inc., NOVA Chemicals, and the Coal Association of Canada (ISC3 2002).

meetings with the Liberal MPs should be timed strategically to ensure that Kyoto ratification is raised as a topic of discussion at this meeting. It was noted that the caucus meeting program, which includes a golf tournament open to outsiders on Monday, August 19, may also offer an opportunity for industry representatives to meet informally with key Liberal MPs on this file. (ISC3 2002, 4)

Although the minutes do note that representatives from the Department of Natural Resources continued to be "supportive of industry views," there was clear concern that others within government "had made up their minds and are pushing forward on this file." Specifically, continued attempts by industry to undermine the credibility of the science appeared to have little effect on government officials, particularly those from Environment Canada (ISC3 2002).

In early September, industry was given yet another reason to worry. At the United Nations Conference on Environment and Development, Prime Minister Chrétien announced that a resolution on the ratification of the Kyoto Protocol would be voted on in the House of Commons before the end of the year. This surprised many, both because the government had given no indication of such an announcement in advance and because in Canada international treaties are ratified by cabinet, not by a vote in the House. With his cabinet divided on the issue, however, Chrétien looked to the House for support with the view that, if it voted in favour of ratification, cabinet could hardly refuse to do so (Harrison 2007). For the business community, the announcement upped the ante, changing the venue of advocacy by providing far more power to backbench MPs than usual. Industry consequently shifted gears, looking to the Canadian public for support.

On 10 September a full-page ad appeared in the *Globe and Mail* announcing industry's views in favour of a "made-in-Canada" approach (Macdonald 2003). On 26 September came the announcement of the creation of a coalition of thirty-two business organizations, the Canadian Coalition for Responsible Environmental Solutions (CCRES). In its inaugural press release, the group again called for a "made-in-Canada" approach to climate change policy, similar to the one outlined by the CCCE in June (Macdonald 2003). The coalition's plan had five "key points," focused on subsidies and voluntary agreements:

- recognition for past, present, and future climate change actions to ensure that those who acted early are rewarded, rather than penalized;

- negotiated agreements with specific economic sectors on emissions performance targets;
- enhanced education and consumer awareness campaigns aimed at energy conservation;
- incentives for generators of renewable energy, those who invest in these clean energy sources, and consumers who upgrade to cleaner sources from older technology; and
- consideration of Canada's trade relationship with the United States and the country's membership in the North American Free Trade Agreement in order to ensure its ongoing competitiveness (CCRES 2002).

Over the following two months, CCRES representatives, led by those from CAPP and the CCCE, wrote letters to high-level officials, appeared before Parliament, created websites in both official languages, and began a major television campaign (Macdonald 2003). Nonetheless, the shift, if minor, in government policy in favour of regulation was confirmed when the Liberals released yet another implementation plan in November. Unlike previous plans, the document linked subsidies to "covenants, with a regulatory or financial backstop, and emissions trading with access to domestic offsets and international permits" for large final emitters (Canada 2002b). Despite a large expenditure of effort and money, however, the CCRES was ultimately unsuccessful in its founding objective. Following the passing of a House of Commons resolution in favour of ratification on 10 December, cabinet ratified the Kyoto Protocol on 13 December 2002.

Although the government had never before backed up its policy declarations with promises of regulation, the environmental plan of 2002 hardly represented a watershed moment in Canadian environmental policy. Covenants with regulatory backstops are perhaps best described as voluntary agreements with (possible) bite and, therefore, represent only a minor shift along the continuum of climate change policy instruments. Nonetheless, it was the first time the government had planned the adoption of emissions trading, which in itself was a departure from the past. At the time, the majority industry preference articulated by the CCRES and CCCE was generally for covenants, but they avoided discussion of emissions trading or other compliance mechanisms.

The one notable and unexpected exception came from CAPP, which appeared far more ready to adopt the government's language of covenants with regulatory backstops and offsets. In a letter to two Atlantic

Canadian ministers on 18 November, three days before the release of the government's plan, CAPP's president and chairman wrote: "We believe that our industry can negotiate with the two levels of government and agree on sector plans and the associated regulatory backstops" (Alvarez and Dielwart 2002). The letter preceded this declaration with a discussion of the role that offsets should play in the system. As I discuss below, CAPP was then in private consultations with the government, which might have given it reason for optimism about the capacity of industry and government to negotiate and agree.

The Deal: Autumn 2002

Publicly, it appeared that business and government could agree on little in the fall of 2002; privately, however, they managed to come to an accord. In a letter to CAPP chairman John Dielwart dated 18 December, five days after ratification, Natural Resources Minister Herb Dhaliwal wrote: "On the price of carbon credits, the government will ensure that, during the first commitment period, Canadian companies will be able to meet their emission reduction and responsibilities at a price no greater than $15 a tonne … With respect to the volume of emissions, the government will set the emissions intensity targets for the oil and gas sector at a level not more than 15 percent below projected business-as-usual levels for 2010" (Dhaliwal 2002). The letter articulated a deal between CAPP and the highest levels of government to limit the industry's future emissions liabilities. In September 2002, facing extreme protests from the business community, Prime Minister Chrétien had ordered his deputy, the clerk of the privy council, with the support and assistance of Alberta regional minister Anne McLellan to begin private negotiations with the petroleum industry (Harrison 2010). Although no formal agreement was ever signed, the letter, according to former CAPP president Pierre Alvarez, represented a negotiated settlement between the government and the petroleum sector that subsequently was extended to all industrial sectors.

The deal is generally perceived as a coup for industry because projections at the time suggested that a price on carbon of between $100 and $250 per tonne would be required to ensure compliance. It therefore made it impossible for Canada to meet its Kyoto Protocol obligations without massive public spending on international credits or domestic subsidies (Harrison 2007). Why Chrétien would have agreed to a plan that effectively undercut the Kyoto Protocol after fighting so hard for ratification was unclear at the time. Chapter 5 returns to this issue.

The Natural Resources Canada Years: 2003–04

In the wake of the agreement with industry, Prime Minister Chrétien appointed National Resources Canada as the lead department on climate change under Deputy Minister George Anderson. In November 2002, Anderson tapped Howard Brown, a former director general at the Department of Finance, to develop regulations. While Brown's group moved forward on policy options, no policy instrument plan made it past the proposal stage at this time. One former government official questioned the prime minister's support for regulation, as many proposals were sent to cabinet but never implemented. Nonetheless, during this period, Natural Resources Canada was in consultation with industry on a system that would include binding covenants (negotiated agreements) with an emissions-trading component.

Despite the agreement with the government, the oil industry quickly returned to a state of pessimism and hostility where climate change policy was concerned. In the February/March 2003 issue of the magazine *HazMat Management*, CAPP president Pierre Alvarez lamented the Kyoto Protocol's effect on competitiveness: "Canada is the only country with a growing energy sector that is forcing the industry to absorb an additional financial burden associated with reducing emissions. The result will be to add more costs on hydrocarbon basins that are already some of the highest cost places to produce oil and gas in the global market. Any extra cost can make an industry uncompetitive internationally." Alvarez argued that, instead of purchasing foreign credits, "energy innovation, research and development programs hold far more promise" (cited in Crittenden 2003). In other words, for CAPP, in early 2003, subsidies remained the preferred instrument.

The CCCE also showed no support for regulation. Appearing in front of the Standing Senate Committee on Energy, the Environment and Natural Resources, CCCE representative John Dillon argued in favour of negotiated agreements between government and industry based on "what is technically and economically feasible in those sectors," but he said nothing about the regulatory backstop that the government had argued would accompany such agreements. Instead, Dillon argued that government should compel industry only to become as efficient as possible given current technology (Dillon 2003).

Over time, however, industry preferences did appear to shift in response to government policy changes, at least among some individual firms. In fall 2003, the government signed a Memorandum of

Understanding with each of the Forest Products Association of Canada (FPAC), Dupont Chemicals, and the International Emissions Trading Association (IETA). All three memoranda laid out the principles involved in a potential emissions-trading system. A number of Canadian companies supported the IETA agreement, including TransAlta, Suncor Energy, Petro-Canada, Shell Canada, St. Lawrence Cement, ConocoPhillips Canada, and Abitibi-Consolidated. Although the agreed-upon principles were generally broad and related to harmonization with other international emissions-trading systems, as well as with the general principles of a well-functioning market, they demonstrated an acceptance on the part of a wider number of firms that emissions trading within Canada was likely.

Nonetheless, the majority of firms and associations remained hostile to regulation. Mike Bradley, then chair of the climate change committee of the FPAC, remembered his industry's being isolated from other business groups at the time. Only Dupont, from his perspective, was as open to emissions trading as the forestry industry. Avrim Lazar, FPAC's president, saw his group's position as a significant break from the business consensus: "We completely separated from the [other] groups and they weren't happy with us, but we weren't happy with them either."

The Dion Years: 2004–06

Immediately following Paul Martin's becoming prime minister in December 2003, little changed in the realm of climate change policy. After the subsequent election in June 2004, however, Martin appointed former intergovernmental affairs minister Stéphane Dion as environment minister. Over the following year, according to a former advisor, Dion lobbied hard to have the climate change file moved from Natural Resources Canada to his department, and succeeded when he was appointed to chair a cabinet committee on climate change in 2005. The environment department subsequently drafted regulations, including intensity targets for large final emitters, emissions trading, and a technology fund for partial compliance.

In April 2005 the government launched "Moving Forward on Climate Change: A Plan for Honouring Our Kyoto Commitments." The new plan included a regulatory cap-and-trade program, but it continued to rely substantially on public spending. Strenuously omitted from the plan were estimates on the cost and quantity of international credits that would be needed to meet Canada's Kyoto Protocol commitments

(Harrison 2010). Although industry had supported the previous Chrétien government in its push for flexible mechanisms in the late 1990s
and early 2000s, by 2005 such policies had fallen out of favour, both
within government and without. As interview subject John Drexhage, a
former government negotiator, explained:

> Something funny happened on the way to ratification. You got the ...
> NGOs who kept on talking about these things as just being a bunch of
> loopholes, [saying], all the reductions should be at home, etc. And then
> industry thought about this a bit more and they said, well, hold on, why
> should all this money go oversees? Why instead shouldn't we put it
> towards the development of our own technologies? [They made] it sort
> of an either/or kind of thing. Particularly, Paul Martin heard this com-
> ing from both sides – from the NGOs and the business community – and
> thought, well, that's a no-brainer, I'll be for this too, without appreciat-
> ing the fact that he was painting the government into a very tight corner
> because a) it takes time for technology [to develop] and b) there is only so
> much that can be done domestically, certainly in the timeframe of 2012.

International mechanisms, therefore, went unmentioned in the published plan. With a 100 megatonne shortfall between compliance and
stated emissions reductions, however, it remained likely, if unacknowl-
edged, that such mechanisms would be required (Harrison 2010).

Notwithstanding the government's obfuscation with respect to international mechanisms, there was considerable progress towards the
adoption of regulatory mechanisms that year. In July the government
published a "Notice of Intent to Regulate" in the *Canada Gazette*, the
most substantial indication to that date that it was serious about regulation (Canada 2005). In November it upped the ante, adding carbon
dioxide to the list of toxic substances under the Canadian Environmental Protection Act (CEPA), an action that provided the necessary legislative authority for the regulatory framework to follow. Former aides,
including senior policy advisor Dahlia Stein, told me that Dion planned
for the final regulations to be published in January 2006.

Despite Dion's clear push for regulation, his plans were not without their limitations. A bizarre debate and minor capitulation followed
the government's introduction on 24 March 2005 of Bill C-43, a budget
implementation bill. Section 15 of the bill would have removed the
word "toxic" from CEPA. The intention was ultimately to include carbon dioxide in the list of controlled substances without having to face

the scrutiny that undoubtedly would have followed, given that CO_2 is found in our very breath. The move attracted attention and concern among the ENGO and legal communities, however, and was characterized by the Conservative opposition as a backdoor channel for implementing a carbon tax (Fishlock and Mercer 2005). Environmentalists and law experts later expressed concern that the change would make the act unconstitutional (Freeman 2006). Ultimately, the government removed the reference from the budget and later listed CO_2 as toxic anyway.

In addition to this challenge, Dion lost a fight in cabinet to regulate the auto industry in relation to emissions standards; the winner was Natural Resources Canada, which favoured further use of voluntary agreements (Harrison 2010). Consequently, although there is no doubt that, in early 2006, Dion also wanted to introduce standards for stationary sources of emissions, his ability to get cabinet to agree to such regulations remained questionable.

During this period, most business actors continued to be hostile to regulatory instruments. The day after the government unveiled its new climate change plan in April 2005, the CCCE issued a press release decrying the government's continued focus on meeting its Kyoto targets. The release again called for a "more innovative, made-in-Canada approach," but provided few details on what that would involve, stating only that such an approach should "develop new technologies" (CCCE 2005).

Industry's lack of clear public declaration for any policy instrument at the time, however, masked continued support for voluntary agreements and subsidies. In January 2005 the president of the Canadian Chemical Producers' Association (CCPA), Richard Paton, wrote to Dion arguing in favour of a Memorandum of Understanding between the chemical industry and the government, not to support a regulatory cap-and-trade program, but in place of "permitting or other climate change legislative or regulatory measures" (Paton 2005a).

In September Paton again wrote to Dion, this time arguing against the inclusion of carbon in the list of toxic chemicals under CEPA. As the government had anticipated when it attempted to remove "toxic" from the act the previous spring, the CCPA's complaint resulted from the perceived foolishness of referring to CO_2 as toxic: "It would be inappropriate for CO_2 to be labeled as toxic under CEPA. Just as Cabinet recognized that it would be inappropriate and confusing to the public to label road salt as toxic, the same conclusion should be reached for CO_2,"

(Paton 2005b). Despite this and other interventions, Dion succeeded in adding CO_2 to the list in November.

According to senior staff in the minister's office at that time, the CCPA was not alone in its views, particularly in its distrust of regulation. As a former advisor to the minister told me in 2009, "No one was saying regulate [in 2004–05]. Everybody was saying, 'let's keep it voluntary. We're taking voluntary action. Trust us. Trust us.'" Another senior staff member agreed: "They didn't like it. They did not want to be regulated." Industry continued to extol the virtues of voluntary programs until the Liberal government was defeated in early 2006.

The Harper Government: 2006

In December 2005 Prime Minister Martin lost a vote of non-confidence in the House of Commons, then lost the subsequent general election. Conservative leader Stephen Harper, who became prime minister in January 2006, previously had made clear his scepticism about climate change, and during his first six months in office abandoned all of the previous government's climate policies (Harrison 2010). When the Harper government put out its own "made-in-Canada" plan in October 2006 in the guise of the Clean Air Act, it focused primarily on conventional air pollutants, and planned merely to stop the growth of carbon emissions by 2025.

Given that a "made-in-Canada plan" had first been proposed by the CCCE in 2002, it is understandable that, in early 2006, most in the business community thought that the threat of regulation had subsided, according to Tony Macerollo of the Canadian Petroleum Products Institute. Industry's first strategy in the new political environment was to reconfirm its support of voluntary agreements and subsidies. In summer 2006 the CCCE drafted a memorandum for the new environment minister, Rona Ambrose, in which it claimed it would "stand ready to support a '*made-in-Canada*' plan that makes measurable progress in addressing greenhouse gas emissions from all segments of Canadian society." This policy should not, however, resemble the "flawed" policies of the previous government: "After many years of paying lip-service to a flawed international agreement and funneling taxpayers' dollars into dead-end schemes, it is time for a serious discussion about what Canadians are actually prepared to do, and how best to spend valuable resources, both private and public, to achieve sustainable and lasting solutions" (CCCE 2006, 1–2; emphasis in original). The focus of the rest of the document was on developing incentives for investment in clean technology, the need for public-private partnerships for technological growth, and the need for feasible and effective targets. As of July 2006, therefore, the CCCE's preferences had not changed substantially from those articulated during the ratification debate of 2002, a point that is made explicit in the opening paragraph of the memorandum: "The Council first issued its strategy and recommendations on a '*made-in-Canada*' climate change policy in 2002. Some of our fundamental thinking from that time remains unchanged" (CCCE 2006, 1; emphasis in original).

By the time the Conservatives announced their plan in October, however, the political landscape had changed. The public, which had been largely inattentive to environmental issues since 1992, suddenly became interested and concerned. In the fourth quarter of 2005, when the Conservatives were running their winning election campaign, only 6.4 per cent of respondents to an Environics poll viewed the environment as the most important problem facing the country, while 27.7 per cent believed health care was the most significant problem. By the first quarter of 2006, the environment had vaulted into a close second place (21.5 per cent) behind health care (22.0 per cent). By the second quarter, environment/pollution was the most cited "problem," remaining in first or close second place until 2008. By fall 2006, then, the business community and the Harper government both found themselves offside with the public.

The shift in public opinion was precipitated by a number of events in 2005 and 2006. First, the devastation caused by Hurricane Katrina in New Orleans in September 2005 provided environmentalists with an image to attach to the previously abstract concept of climate change, a practice that was common by summer 2006. Also, in the summer 2006, Al Gore's movie, *An Inconvenient Truth*, attracted popular attention to the cause, eventually winning an Academy Award in early 2007. Suddenly, popular celebrities such as Oprah Winfrey were focused on climate change. This public attention was augmented by the release in the United Kingdom that fall of the Stern report on the economics of climate change (Stern 2006).

The public mood in favour of action on climate change clearly influenced business preferences. The CCCE might still have been dissembling about regulation in July, but by November 2006 it was being forceful and clear. Testifying before the House of Commons Standing Committee on Environment and Sustainable Development, CCCE representative John Dillon declared: "Industry is not opposed to regulation, as many of our critics have tended to suggest" (Dillon 2006). Despite the implication that support of regulation had been a long-time industry policy, this was the first indication the CCCE had ever given publicly that it, or its members, would accept the implementation of a regulatory instrument.

A Climate of Change: 2007–08

Having fully digested the public's mood, governments – both provincial and federal – began to propose concrete regulatory frameworks in 2007. At the federal level, the government replaced its rookie environment minister in January 2007 and in April announced a new regulatory plan, "Turning the Corner." Almost a year later, in March 2008, more details were provided. The program looked similar to the previous government's regulatory framework: intensity targets for large final emitters on a sectoral or facility basis (depending on the industry), domestic emissions trading to reach targets, and a limited compliance technology fund at $15 per tonne. The technology fund component was to be phased out by 2018 (Canada 2008).

At the provincial level, Quebec was the first to act with a very limited $3 per tonne carbon tax in 2006. A more substantial carbon-pricing program came in 2007 from an unlikely source, Alberta, when that government implemented the regulatory framework developed by the federal Liberals during Stéphane Dion's tenure. The Alberta program, however, included two adaptations: emissions credits could be bought only for projects in Alberta, and there was no limit on compliance through a technology fund at $15 per tonne. As a result, given the lack of sellers of credits in Alberta, a program that on the surface appears to be cap-and-trade actually acts as a carbon tax on emissions above a set quota. It is, therefore, a hybrid of the two systems. At $15 per tonne, however, the program still represents one of the most substantial carbon prices in North America to date.

British Columbia announced its high-profile carbon tax in February 2008. The tax, which took effect on 1 July 2008, charged all consumers of fossil fuels $10 per tonne of CO_2 and scheduled an annual increase of $5 per tonne of CO_2 until 2012, when the tax would be $30 per tonne. British Columbia also put in place legislation for a planned cap-and-trade system as part of the Western Climate Initiative to cover emissions by "designated large emitters" (British Columbia 2008).

Initially British Columbia's carbon tax was well received, and in June 2008 the federal Liberals followed suit, announcing their "Green Shift," a proposal for a revenue-neutral carbon tax. Unfortunately for the Liberals, gas prices increased drastically in the first half of 2008 and the policy instrument quickly became unpopular. In the October 2008 general election, the party received its lowest vote share to that date in Canadian history, at 26 per cent. Whether this was due to the carbon tax, the party's unpopular leader (Dion), or the economic crisis that erupted that fall, it was clear that carbon taxation would be relegated to the political wilderness at the federal level in the near future. In British Columbia, however, the tax passed the test of the next provincial election and remains in place (Harrison 2009). During this period, other provinces also announced the development of regulatory instruments, while Quebec, Ontario, Manitoba, and British Columbia joined the Western Climate Initiative, pledging to develop a cap-and-trade system by 2012.

At the time, business preferences also shifted decidedly in favour of carbon pricing. Although the CCCE appeared to have shifted its preference in favour of regulation in late 2006, CAPP took more time. On 12 February 2007, Rick Hyndman, CAPP's climate change advisor, was quoted as stating: "sticking with the kinds of policy that we've been discussing – targets for emissions intensity improvements and investment in technology – is the right way to go. So neither a full-blown carbon tax or international emission trading makes sense at this point" (Hyndman, cited in Burrows 2007). Two months later, however, in a presentation to CIBC World Markets, Hyndman extolled the virtues of a global carbon tax, and CAPP has supported a carbon tax-like policy instrument ever since. The instrument design would see the industry pay a set price on emissions above a set quota, which makes the proposal a hybrid of cap-and-trade and taxation. Further, CAPP argues that all money collected should be returned to industry for green initiatives in the same industry that paid the "tax," another variation on the standard "revenue-neutral" taxation framework.

Other industries also appear to have gone through a similar shift during the period from 2006 to early 2008. For instance, when Cliff Mackay became president of the Railway Association of Canada (RAC) in May 2006, the association had made no clear statement on climate change policy instruments. Mackay, however, asked for a "white paper" on policy instruments, and the white paper's support of cap-and-trade was approved by the RAC's board late that same year and became "the policy of the industry." Many other interview subjects remembered a shift in the way industry thought of climate change around the same time. For Tony Macerollo of the Canadian Petroleum Products Institute, for instance, "fate was sealed, the door was shut roughly around December 2006, 2007, maybe where the last remaining non-engagers recognized that they had to engage." Forestry industry representatives, who were to some extent external observers of the majority business preference, also date the shift to 2006. According to Mike Bradley of Canfor and former chair of the FPAC's climate change committee, "there was certainly a change in the mood of the public which would probably date from around 2006 and [business] people started waking up to the reality that things are going to change, what is the best way for us to cope in a world where we have this carbon constraint … and that's circa 2006."

Waiting for Obama: 2008–09

Public attention to environmental issues began to wane in 2008, particularly in response to high gas prices, which became the "most important problem" in the second quarter of the year. After the eruption of the economic crisis during the 2008 federal election and the subsequent election of Barack Obama as president in the United States, the Canadian government delayed its planned regulations. The government claimed both that it was delaying due to the economic crisis and that it was waiting for the new US administration to create a continental policy instrument (McCarthy and Galloway 2010; Rennie 2009). Surprisingly, despite the decrease in pressure from government, the business community remained strongly in favour of carbon pricing in 2009. Variation, however, existed in the type of carbon price supported.

The industry preference at the time I conducted the interviews for this study was clearly against further delay. As Lehigh's Brent Korobanik explained, "the big thing here is that we just want to know what we're facing and get on with it." Other business leaders – for example, CAPP's Rick Hyndman and the FPAC's Avrim Lazar – made a similar case, decrying the lack of certainty around policy created by the federal government's continued delays. Officials at Environment Canada confirmed industry's displeasure about further postponements. As one government official explained, "The fact that the US administration is changing, our minister is changed, government changed; there is a transition process now that we are wading through. Our political system, federally, … has had so much transition over the past three years; it is very frustrating for them as stakeholders because they are not getting the certainty that they need to be able to make their decisions. It's very, very frustrating for them."

Interestingly, since that time much has changed in climate politics in North America. The Canadian government continued to wait for US action, which remained likely – and was ongoing in Congress – until April 2010, when the best chance for a US cap-and-trade program collapsed in the Senate. The Democrats' loss of control of Congress in November 2010 extinguished any hope for a resuscitation of carbon pricing in the United States in the near term (Lizza 2010). This, coupled with the Canadian government's continued unwillingness to act unilaterally, has meant that, unlike in 2009, carbon pricing was no longer viewed as inevitable in either Washington or Ottawa. Equally, the regulatory difficulties faced by proponents of the Keystone pipeline, which was opposed by US environmentalists largely due to the carbon content of oil sands petroleum, continued to demonstrate the significance of climate change for US and Canadian energy companies. With the end of the Harper era in 2015, firms once again faced the prospect of near-term carbon pricing. This likelihood became all but certain when the Trudeau government announced in September 2016 that it would impose a carbon price on any province that did not develop its own system. Thus, the regulatory environment has oscillated substantially since 2009, when the scope of this research forces a conclusion to this historical review, but it has now settled back to pre-recession expectations of action.

Summary of Findings

Government policy variations on climate change and the pattern of business preferences for climate change policy instruments over the period from 1988 to 2009 are plotted chronologically in Figure 1. Policy instruments proposed by government are arranged on an ordinal scale on the Y axis by level of coercion and (roughly) theoretical cost to business, with cap-and-trade and carbon taxation lumped together, as they were generally seen by businesses as alternative forms of carbon pricing. Interpretation was required to determine the placement of business preferences and government policy at a number of points, particularly for business in 2002 and for government in 2006 and 2008. At these points, the placement represents a simplification of policy or preference. Nonetheless, the graph is useful as a tool of analysis in illustrating changes over time.

Public attention to environmental issues can also be summarized in graphical form, using responses from Environic's "Most Important Issue" question (see Figure 2). The question provides a good proxy

Figure 1. Business Preferences and Government Policy Instruments on
Climate Change, Canada, 1988–2009

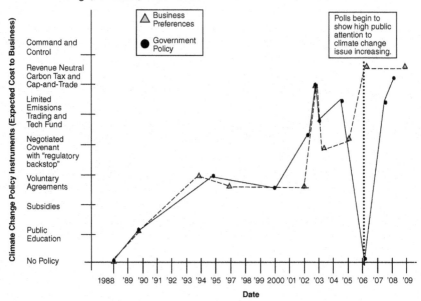

Source: Author's compilation.

for public attention, as it demonstrates both the relative importance of environmental issues compared to other salient issues over time. From 1988 to 2009, four issues vied for top spot in this poll: unemployment, economy/money/interest, health care, and pollution/environment. The environment broke through the noise and became the top concern of a plurality of respondents in two periods: 1989–90 and 2006–07.

Figures 1 and 2 help illustrate five points about business preferences for climate change policy instruments in relation to government policy declarations and public opinion since the late 1980s.

First, despite small pockets of dissent, there was a remarkable amount of homogeneity in business preferences during the entire period from 1989 to 2009, although after 2006 there was variation in the type of market mechanism (carbon price) supported.

Second, from the early 1990s to 2006, business overwhelmingly supported voluntary agreements and subsidies to deal with climate change. Business actors generally articulated their disapproval with

Figure 2. The Most Important Problem Facing Canada Today: Poll Results, 1988–2009, by Year and Quarter

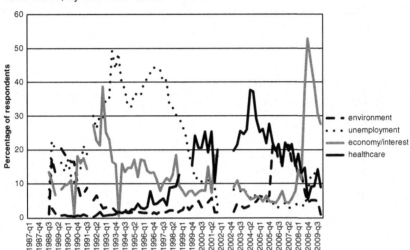

Sources: Environics, *Environmental Monitor*, 4th quarter 1992; Environics, *Focus Canada*, various issues.

regulatory policies, whether traditional or market mechanisms, due to the increased costs they would entail, particularly vis-à-vis global competitors. Government movement towards limited emissions trading and somewhat (although slightly) more coercive policies after 2004 did not elicit an immediate change in aggregate business preference.

Third, a clear change in business preference away from voluntary agreements and subsidies in favour of carbon pricing was first discernible in late 2006, the same year as a shift in public attention towards the issue. Indeed, business actors, particularly industry leader CCCE, appeared at least as or possibly more attentive to public opinion than did government, first demonstrating a shift in rhetoric in November 2006 while the federal government was still defending its much-maligned Clean Air Act. Indeed, although the Conservative government that came to power in 2006 was sceptical about climate change, industry became more, not less, progressive in its stance that year. The overall shift in preference within the greater business community, however, took place over the following six to eight months (late 2006-mid 2007) and corresponded with a time when both industry and government were adapting to the increased significance of climate change as a policy issue.

Fourth, industry did not explain why the rhetoric it previously employed against market mechanisms – that they would increase costs for Canadian firms in relation to those of competitor countries, decreasing Canada's competitiveness – was no longer deemed valid. This is particularly striking given that the business community was not generally calling for the federal government to wait for the United States, despite the government's insistence on doing so in 2009.

Fifth, although business preference for climate change policy instruments changed just as public attentiveness to environmental issues was at its height, industry did not shift back to a preference for voluntary agreements and subsidies once public attentiveness waned in 2008.

In the end, however, the question of what caused large businesses in Canada to shift their preference away from voluntary agreements and subsidies when they did cannot be answered through a simple historical review. What can be said is that the shift correlates with a time of heightened public attention to the environment, one of only two such times since 1988. This suggests that firms' preferences are not apolitical or exogenous to the political process, but are affected by changes in the political sphere. In particular, it appears that the increased public attention to the policy area influenced business preference for climate change policy instruments, just as it did government action.

Although the correlation between public attention to environmental issues and a shift in business preference is interesting, the more notable question is: Why did business preference shift at the same time as public attention to environmental issues was at its highest? Did public concern itself cause the shift, or was some other variable also influenced by public opinion? If public opinion itself was the cause of this shift, why did firms' preferences not shift back to voluntary agreements and subsidies once public attentiveness waned?

From a risk-advantage perspective, of course, the answers to these questions rest with the connections among public concern or attentiveness, expectations of future policy instrument implementation by governments, and investors' concerns. Even the abandonment of the cost argument highlighted in point four above makes sense: industry would be expected to use every possible argument in favour of the status quo regulatory environment, only accepting minor changes (voluntary agreements and subsidies) until the stability of that environment could no longer be relied upon. This tipping point happened when public opinion shifted in 2006–07 and managers began to believe that regulatory mechanisms were inevitable in dealing with climate change. At that time, the prerogative shifted from supporting the now-uncertain status quo to ensuring the adoption of the expected policy instruments as soon as possible, thus creating a new, stable regulatory environment.

Regulatory (in)stability is significant, not just because firms require stability to invest, but because instability increases risk (and the perception thereof) for external investors. Since external investors are a diverse and diffuse group, I argue that firms *also* look to public opinion as an indicator of investors' concerns, and that this link between public opinion and investors helps explain the observed correlation between public attentiveness and business preferences. If the public is highly attentive to climate change as a policy problem, then the subset of the public that invests, the investor class, is also likely aware of the problem and alert to the possibility of regulatory change. Firms then need to respond to the issue by assuring their investors they can survive a regulatory change. They do this, in part, by supporting the policy change and arguing for its implementation as soon as possible.

More evidence is required, however, to support this claim. In this chapter I have merely demonstrated the correlation between high public attentiveness to the environment in 2006–07 and a shift in business preference for climate change policy instruments during the same period. In Chapter 5 I take on the task of demonstrating, using evidence other than the interviews from which the model was developed, that investors' concerns are key to understanding this link.

Chapter Five

Legitimacy, Public Opinion, and Investment

Why does public opinion matter to firms? This question is not only significant for understanding the findings of this study; it is also, as I discussed in Chapter 2, relevant to previous work in business-government relations on environmental policy in Canada. Macdonald (2007) argues that firms are motivated by their thirst for legitimacy (public support) in creating their public policy preferences, but he does not explain why they care about public perception. I argue that public opinion matters to business in part because it acts as a clear indicator of investors', particularly shareholders', concerns. In this chapter I present evidence to support this argument. If firms do indeed respond to public opinion in part because shareholders are a subset of that public, then they ought to respond by changing the way in which they communicate with shareholders after a shift in public opinion has occurred. The evidence I present here demonstrates that this shift was indeed apparent in a central medium through which firms communicate with shareholders: the annual report. The annual reports of the firms that participated in my study support the contention of interview subjects that assuaging shareholders' and large capital investors' concerns was a key motivator in the development of policy instrument preferences. Indeed, interview subjects argued that investors' concerns even explain a peculiar story in the history of business-government relations on climate change in Canada: the 2002 deal between the federal government and the Canadian Association of Petroleum Producers (CAPP).

Certainly, interview subjects left little doubt that investment was top of mind for business leaders when analysing climate change policy instruments. As the president of the Canadian Chemical Producers' Association, Richard Paton, explained: "It reflects the nature of our industry. Most investments in our kind of industry – same with steel, mining, and forestry – they're thirty-year investments, so you don't want to be doing something and then find out ten years later that society has decided that this is not a good thing to be doing, because it's just too expensive to change the plant. So, what you want to do is to anticipate what society wants and consequently work on a balanced approach that gives you, what we call in Responsible Care – a licence to operate." For industry, one of the greatest challenges of the climate change regulatory environment – in particular, the lack of certainty about government policy instrument choices and implementation – is that it undermines firms' capacity to plan and, therefore, to make large-scale investments.

Adding insult to injury is that the firms most affected by climate change policy are also those most impacted by policy uncertainty, since the most energy-intensive firms also tend to have the longest-term capital stock investments. For some firms the worst-case climate policy scenario could completely undermine their business model and threaten their survival. Robert Page, chair of the National Round Table on the Environment and the Economy and former senior executive at TransAlta, a coal-generated power company based in Calgary, explained: "If the government of Canada says five years from now coal-fired power generation will cease in this country, you're done. And, yes, your other wind power and natural gas and others can keep going, but you've got a locked in investment there and you suddenly have a stranded asset." According to Page, during his time at TransAlta, the possibility that governments in Canada or the United States would one day ban coal-fired generation was a real and serious concern that animated the company's climate change strategy. Since TransAlta previously had invested substantially in coal, such a ban could threaten its expected return on investments, although the company's ability to survive would depend on the details of the ban, including any phase-out period and timing vis-à-vis the lifespan of current investments.

The chance that today's investment will become "stranded" tomorrow is at the very heart of the concept of risk for business leaders. Avoiding this possibility with respect to climate change policy instruments requires a stable and long-term regulatory framework, otherwise firms will be unwilling to make the large investments that are commonplace in heavy industry. In 2009 oil firm Nexen, for instance, delayed the second phase of its oil sands development at Long Lake, Alberta, because of uncertainty over climate change regulation (Blackwell 2009).

Although Nexen expanded the project in 2014, the company noted in its 2010 annual report: "Any required reductions in the greenhouse gases ... emitted from our operations (without an allowed offset compliance mechanism) could result in increases to our capital or operating expense, or reduced operating rates, especially at the Long Lake project, which could have an adverse effect on our results of operations and financial condition" (Nexen 2010).

The dilatory effects of policy uncertainty on long-term investment causes business leaders to pay considerable attention to policy trends, to try to "read the tea leaves" as much as possible. As a former senior official at Gaz Métro explained:

> When you are in businesses that work on a long-term basis, their screen to the future integrates emerging trends and they have to take good note of it because the investors do and the investors ask questions and they say, "what do you intend to do about this?" So, you have to address these issues. Addressing issues is short term, but addressing trends that start emerging is something that you have to do because you are talking about billions of dollars of investments in the future. So, I would venture to say that large industry is very sensitive, very permeable, to those kinds of evolving trends and they start factoring them in much earlier than we suspect.

As the quote implies, the internal investments discussed above are unavoidably linked to the second type of investment: those made in the firm by shareholders and institutional investors. The risk assessments of these two groups are significant, since without financial investment industries are unable to grow. Moreover, firms compete for investment with other firms in the global marketplace and, therefore, must ensure that they are perceived as a safe vehicle for investment capital. As the president of the Mining Association of Canada, Gordon Peeling, argued to a House of Commons committee in 2002: "Capital is very mobile, and if it can earn a better return on resource development outside of Canada, it will flow to those jurisdictions with no Kyoto obligations. That's just not Canadian capital, that is New York capital, Zurich capital, London capital – all those markets this industry goes to for both investment purposes here in Canada, and investment purposes and opportunities outside of Canada" (Peeling 2002). Shareholders can also influence corporate decision-making by withholding investment. Not only can retail shareholders choose to move en masse away from a firm; large shareholder blocks, such as pension funds, can also cause significant damage to a firm's share value. As Robert Page noted, "the Ontario Teachers' Pension [Plan] was the second largest shareholder in TransAlta during the years that I was there, and the Canada Pension [Plan] was the largest. If these pension funds start getting complaints from all their members that we are not good corporate citizens, then those pension funds begin to feel the pressure that the continuance of their contracts are going to be challenged in connection with that." Interestingly, withholding funding is not the only manner in which investors influence corporate action. Shareholders can have a significant impact on corporate governance, a power that is less often wielded, but nonetheless top-of-mind for some. As an official at Shell Canada said, "There are blocks now of shareholders that have a lot of influence and if they don't like what a company is doing, they are going to voice their opinion and they are going, if necessary, to change the board."

Canadian business leaders paint a picture in which investment is a constant concern for senior executives, ensuring both that the company is in a position to make long-term investments and that external investors are satisfied with the company's ability to provide stable and expected returns. Climate change policy is one area that can undermine investor confidence and, therefore, business success. Business preferences for government policy instruments, consequently, are created with one eye on limiting the risks to investment. John Dillon of the Canadian Council of Chief Executives discussed the issue while testifying before Parliament only days before Canada the ratified Kyoto Protocol:

> The most immediate impact of a decision to ratify the Kyoto Protocol would be on business investment, and not just in the oil patch. The federal government has acknowledged that investment is critical to boosting Canadian productivity and incomes, yet Canada would be the only country in the western hemisphere to accept a target, and that alone is likely to push investment to other countries with no targets. Canadians will pay the price but the global climate will see little gain. A move to ratify the Kyoto Protocol without a clear and detailed implementation plan would, we believe, compound this damage. Unless Canadian and international investors are given a clear picture of what new rules will affect business costs in the years ahead, they have to assume that these new costs will be significant. Any uncertainty in the implementation plan adds to the risks of making investments in Canada and is likely to affect not only new investments but also the credit ratings of existing business. (Dillon 2002)

Finally, Avrim Lazar, president of the Forest Products Association of Canada (FPAC), perhaps best summed up the relationship among investment, certainty, and business success: "Because the most critical factor in business success is attracting investment and the thing that investors like the least is unknowable risk, even if the eventual regime won't cost us as much, the ten or fifteen years of uncertainty as to what it will be will cost us enormously. So, knowing what the government's going to do and then having some confidence that they're actually going to do it is our number one priority. Nothing else is as important as that."

The 2002 Deal: Oil Sands Investors and Canadian Climate Policy

It is not, however, just the words of business leaders that highlight the effects of investment and investors on business-government relations. According to both a senior government official and the former president of CAPP, in 2002 third-party investors also had considerable influence on the course of Canadian climate change policy.

In Chapter 3 I briefly discussed the 2002 arrangement between the federal government and CAPP in which the government agreed to cap a future carbon price at $15 per tonne and limit industry's target to 15 per cent below 2010 business-as-usual levels. Natural Resources Minister Herb Dhaliwal made the commitment in a letter to CAPP's chairman only five days after cabinet had ratified the Kyoto Protocol. Since Canada was expected to require a 30 per cent reduction from business-as-usual in 2012 to meet its Kyoto targets and that large final emitters (all of whom were subsequently extended the same assurance) account for about half of Canada's greenhouse gas emissions, the commitment made implementation problematic at best. Moreover, economic analyses at the time suggested that a $150 per tonne price on carbon would be required to reduce emissions to the Kyoto target. As Harrison explains, "the effect of the $15/15 percent guarantee thus was to render it impossible for Canada to comply with the Kyoto Protocol other than through massive public spending on either international credits or domestic subsides to business" (Harrison 2010, 182).

Needless to say, observers were baffled by the government's decision. Why would the Chrétien government make such a seemingly irrational policy choice only days after ratifying the Kyoto Protocol? Macdonald (2003) suggested that the deal resulted from the influence of Natural Resources Canada, as the agreement was made by the department without the knowledge of either Environment Canada or cabinet. As Harrison notes, however, negotiations were conducted between CAPP president Pierre Alvarez, Alberta regional minister Anne McLellan, *and* the prime minister's own deputy, the clerk of the privy council. As a result, although Environment Canada might not have been involved, the agreement clearly had the consent of the prime minister and cannot be explained by a department gone rogue. Another explanation is that the prime minister was forced to make the concession by a concerned cabinet. Harrison argues that the agreement was integral to resolving divisions in cabinet on climate change policy in 2002, and thus played a significant role in ensuring ratification (Harrison 2010). In other words, for Chrétien, settling with the oil and gas industry was a necessary prerequisite to ratification.

Although cabinet concern was undoubtedly a key issue for the prime minister, there was more to the story. It is no coincidence that the deal resulted from negotiations between the government and CAPP, and not any other association. Even though, as AbitibiBowater's Martin Fairbank told me, CAPP was known to be the most hostile to government regulation on climate change and arguably had the most resources to fight the government on the issue, it was forced to negotiate to ensure the continued growth of its industry. At the time, a number of upgrader projects were under development in the oil sands. Upgrading is the process through which bitumen from the oil sands is transformed into synthetic crude oil, which is subsequently refined into gasoline and other petroleum products. Upgraders are usually situated near the source of bitumen in Alberta, but conceivably could be moved to other jurisdictions. These multibillion-dollar facilities require considerable external funding by institutional investors, but in 2002 they were refusing to provide capital without greater certainty about the future price of carbon.

Although most in Ottawa might have viewed it as unlikely that a carbon price would completely undermine the profitability of oil sands production, investors were concerned about ensuring *expected* rates of return, not merely positive rates of return. Thus, the uncertainty of costs matters as much or more than the absolute cost. Although future carbon prices remained undefined by government, the risks of investment were high. This, in turn, made the risk-return trade-off of oil sands projects unpalatable – in other words, the expected returns of the project were not high enough to counteract the increased risk. According to CAPP's then-president Pierre Alvarez and confirmed by a government official close to negotiations, this was the driving force behind the 2002 deal.

Petroleum companies argued that, without greater certainty on this issue, the new upgraders under development would have to be cancelled or moved to areas without climate change targets – for instance, Montana – where funding would be easily acquired. Alberta's oil deposits could not be moved, but the processing plants were relatively mobile, at least at the time of development. As CAPP's Richard Hyndman explained to the House of Commons Standing Committee on Industry, Science and Technology on 11 December 2002:

> Nobody's going to move the [upgrader] plants that are already there, they're not on rollers, but it is a serious consideration for the new oil sands projects where the upgrading hasn't happened. So, somewhere between the bitumen you pull out of the ground and the gasoline that goes into the cars, you have to do the refining, and in the case of Syncrude and Suncor, and now the Shell project that's about to start up, that bitumen is brought up to the quality of light crude oil [in Alberta], which is sent to eastern Canada or central Canada and the U.S. But some of the new projects have a choice as to whether they locate the upgrading part in the U.S. or in Canada, near the production source, and if you're putting costs on doing the upgrading because of the carbon dioxide emissions associated with that energy use in Canada and not in the U.S., that will tip the balance towards locating them in the U.S. (Hyndman 2002)

Indeed, the True North project at Fort Hills, Alberta, was abandoned in 2002 due to factors that included uncertainty over a price on carbon. Although the project's cancellation was not publicly noted until January 2003 (CBC News 2003), Hyndman referred to the project's cancellation during his committee appearance, suggesting the actual decision had been made much earlier. Other projects threatened to follow suit. According to Hyndman, Nexen also delayed a project due to climate change policy uncertainty in 2002.

The postponed developments became an intergovernmental relations headache for the federal government. Alberta understandably was livid about the potential loss of investment and jobs, and called on Ottawa to act. This point is significant: negotiations were not suggested by the prime minister to protect his legacy, but, according to a senior official, undertaken at Alberta's insistence and linked directly to investors' concerns. Negotiations began in September 2002, and by December a deal was struck. With certainty over a future price of carbon of no more than $15 per tonne, investors' risk-return trade-off looked much more palatable, and development continued.

To many observers, this story might seem strange. After all, fluctuations in the price of oil, the Canadian dollar exchange rate, and Alberta labour force costs appear to be greater uncertainties vis-à-vis oil sands development than any possible carbon price. Although the deal appeared irrational for government at first glance and contrary to CAPP's apparent preference, if one takes the influence and interests of third-party investors into account the agreement made sense for both sides.

On CAPP's side, oil companies were literally able to take Dhaliwal's letter to the bank and get the funding to enable growth and increased profits. It is important to note, however, that it was not so much the absolute costs of carbon pricing that mattered, but the uncertainty over those costs and its impact on investment. This explains why no one, including Alvarez, could remember why $15 was chosen as the upper limit of a price on carbon in 2002. The price mattered less than the certainty that the agreement created. With the industry's bankers satisfied, CAPP returned in 2003 to articulating its original preferred policy: voluntary agreements and subsidies. Thus, although CAPP bounded the risk to investors by negotiating the deal, the association did not then materially alter its preference of instrument.

There is, however, one unexplained element of the deal on the business side. The government's commitment to a price no higher than $15 per tonne related only to the "first commitment period" (Dhaliwal 2002), then defined as 2008 to 2012, certainly far shorter than the thirty-to-fifty-year lifespan of most upgrader projects. Why, then, were investors satisfied by the deal? Was it merely because they could not expect a longer-term commitment, given that a future government could change the policy? I obtained no clear response to this question; evidence from interviewees merely demonstrates that investors were indeed satisfied, and tensions waned. This might point to a subjective element in such an interpretation. The concept of anchoring from cognitive psychology – people's habit of biasing a numerical estimate towards a previously available number (in this case, $15) and estimating upward or downward from that number – might provide a possible explanation (see Tversky and Kahneman 1999). The scope of my research, however, did not allow me to pursue that approach. Nonetheless, it appears that once the risks were bounded for the first commitment period, investors felt that the level of risk was low enough in relation to expected returns to warrant the investment. The risk-return trade-off was acceptable at that time.

There is evidence, however, that the perception of certainty or lowered risk with respect to possible future carbon-pricing instruments was, for many business executives, short-lived. By 2009 interview subjects were lamenting the continued uncertainty, and appeared unwilling to trust that future governments would continue the commitments of previous ones. Asked whether he undertook specific cost-benefit analyses of potential climate change policy instruments, Wishart Robson, Nexen's climate change advisor stated:

> There is no ability to do that right now with any sense of confidence because the policy keeps changing and the timelines keep changing. So in December 2002 when Minister Dhaliwal put out his letter from the Government of Canada saying that the program for the Government of Canada would be 15 per cent at a maximum cost of $15 per tonne, the investment community from Lehman Brothers to Moody's came out and they could say "well, that was 22 cents for Suncor, 47cents for Nexen ..." And [since] then [Government has] moved on to so many other things. So ... we now get "Turning the Corner" and then Canada's regulatory framework for air emissions. I stopped after April 2007 – I haven't done a note to our senior management talking in depth about the pros and cons of any policy initiative because it's going to change.

Nonetheless, on the government's side in 2002, the deal prevented a political grenade from exploding in Alberta in the potential loss of billions of dollars in development and thousands of jobs. Dhaliwal made this explicit in the final paragraph of his letter to CAPP: "The Government recognizes such clarity on the cost and volume issues is important for industry to be able to plan and make the investments which will create jobs and increase incomes for Canadians. In providing this clarity, we believe we have addressed a very significant concern for industry and set the stage for a cooperative approach to implementing Canada's Climate Change Plan" (Dhaliwal 2002).

As Harrison found, concessions on the part of government are more likely when jobs will be lost in a specific region (Harrison 1996b). The political power of Alberta as an economic engine for the nation and its treasury further amplified the significance of the problem and increased cabinet's concern. For Alvarez, however, the insistence that government create certainty around possible future carbon prices or jobs in

Alberta would be lost was not a threat, but a market reality. Uncertainty with respect to government policy was affecting investor risk analyses, which influenced business action.

Explaining the 2006 Shift: Public Opinion as an Indicator of Shareholders' Concerns

The accounts that interview subjects offered of the influence of third-party investors on business-government relations provided the foundation for the creation of the risk-advantage model. If this model has broader explanatory power, however, further evidence – independent of the interviews – should indicate a link between investors and business preferences for climate change policy instruments. In particular, the model suggests an explanation for the connection between public opinion and the shift in business preferences in 2006–07 – namely, that firms view public opinion as an indicator of investors' concerns.

I argue that firms care about public opinion both because it indicates the direction of future government policy and because it points to top-of-mind issues for investors, particularly shareholders (or potential shareholders). With respect to the latter, shareholders – like the institutional investors who were so significant in the 2002 deal – choose which firms to invest in by balancing risks and returns. Expectations of future government regulation would be expected to influence their risk perception, but more so when shareholders are aware of an impending change. Since shareholders are a diffuse and diverse group, this most likely would occur when the policy area in question is garnering significant attention in the media. That is, the same forces that were at play in 2002 also might have led to the 2006 shift in preferences, but the characteristics of shareholders as investors (as opposed to institutional investors) mean that firms must infer shareholders' views from some other source – specifically, public opinion.

If public opinion matters to firms because it is an indicator of shareholders' concerns, two correlations should be observable. First, a change in public opinion should have been followed by a clear change in corporate preferences – as in fact did occur, as I demonstrated in Chapter 3. Second, a change in public opinion also should have been followed by a change in the way firms communicated with their shareholders about climate change. In other words, having interpreted the change in public opinion as indicating shareholders' concerns, firms should have responded by addressing those concerns in their communications to shareholders, particularly their annual reports. One way to gauge the extent to which this occurred is to count the number of mentions of climate change in annual reports, which should have increased as firms tried to convince shareholders that climate change policy did not represent a risk to their investment.

Counting "mentions" – that is, every time the term "climate change" is used in an annual report[9] – is a bit of a blunt methodological instrument. After all, the method does not examine the quality of mentions – what the firm was saying when referring to climate change. It also does not take into account differences in writing style – an author who had avoided using the same term repetitively would reduce the number of mentions. Nonetheless, as the number of mentions was counted to create an average across an industry in a given year, and as issues related to writing style should be prevalent in all years, an apparent shift in the average number of mentions over any particular period would suggest a change in the way the firm was communicating with its shareholders. With respect to the quality of those mentions, an examination of the language firms used in relation to climate change also supports this argument, as I discussed in greater detail at the end of the chapter.

Of the three industries I compared, it is in oil and gas that the relationship between public opinion and changes in communications to shareholders should have been the most pronounced. Four of the eight oil and gas firms in the study are publicly traded companies with headquarters in Canada. Their managers, therefore, would have been expected to be both concerned about shareholders' confidence and more sensitive specifically to Canadian public opinion – foreign managers in headquarters abroad would have been far less likely to be aware of, let alone concerned about, Canadian perceptions.

Of the remaining oil and gas firms in the study, two are headquartered in the United States, one in Europe (although it was Canadian until 2006), and one is owned by a partnership of other companies. If my hypothesis holds, the US companies also should have increased the quantity of mentions of climate change in their annual reports, since the issue became salient in that country around the same time. In Europe, however, public concern about climate change increased earlier (Lorenzoni and Pidgeon 2006). Consequently, one would expect oil and gas

---

9   One annual report uses the term "climate protection," rather than "climate change," but those mentions are nevertheless included.

industry annual reports to demonstrate, on average, a clear increase in references to climate change after 2006. Moreover, this increase should be most apparent after the 2006 annual reports, which would have been written in late 2006 and early 2007, before the changes in public opinion and business preferences for policy instruments were complete.

Forestry industry annual reports also should be expected to have increased their mentions of climate change, as four out of the five companies in the study are publicly traded and headquartered in Canada; the exception is the US company Weyerhaeuser. The forestry industry was an early adopter with respect to carbon pricing, however, having supported a cap-and-trade program since 2003, so one would expect the change in their firms' communications to shareholders about climate change to be far less pronounced than in the oil and gas industry. As I discuss in Chapter 5, climate change does not represent as great a risk to investors in the forestry industry as in the gas industry; thus, forestry firms' annual reports should have spent less time on the issue.

Annual reports of the four cement firms in the study, in contrast, should show little or no change in their treatment of climate change. This is not because their Canadian managers were unaware of the change in public opinion, but because all four companies were either wholly owned subsidiaries or arms of much larger foreign corporations, three in Europe and one in Brazil. Their parent companies' reports – written in the company's home country – are unlikely to be influenced by Canadian (or US) public opinion changes, and again, climate change became a salient issue in Europe far earlier, so mentions of it should not have increased after 2006 (Lorenzoni and Pidgeon 2006).

Figures 3, 4, and 5 show the number of mentions of climate change in the annual reports of the three industries from 2001 to 2009.[10]

As expected, in the oil and gas industry, there was a clear change in the number of mentions of climate change in the 2007 annual reports, the year after the public opinion shift began. From 2001 to 2006 mentions of climate change remained relatively constant at approximately 2.4 mentions per annual report. In 2007 the treatment of the subject increased considerably with an average of eight mentions per report.

---

10 The figures were developed from fifty-eight annual reports of seven participating oil and gas companies (Gaz Métro's annual reports were unavailable), forty-three annual reports of five forestry firms, and twenty-one annual reports of three cement firms (annual reports of Essroc and its parent were unavailable).

Figure 3. Mentions of Climate Change in Oil and Gas Firms' Annual Reports, Canada, 2001–09

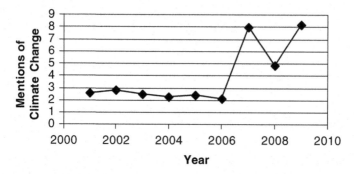

Source: Author's compilation.

Figure 4. Mentions of Climate Change in Forestry Firms' Annual Reports, Canada, 2001–09

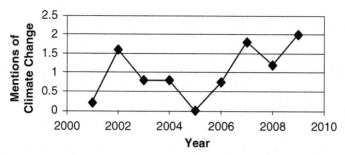

Source: Author's compilation.

Figure 5. Mentions of Climate Change in Cement Firms' Annual Reports, Canada, 2001–09

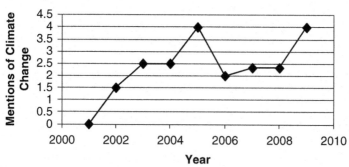

Source: Author's compilation.

This decreased in 2008 to four mentions per report, but, interestingly, despite the focus on the economic crisis that year, mentions of climate change were still two times higher than before 2007. In 2009 climate change mentions returned to an average of eight per report, four times the pre-2007 level.

In the forestry industry, there was also an increase in mentions of climate change after 2007, but, as expected, the change was less pronounced than in the oil and gas industry. Other than in 2002, the year of the ratification of the Kyoto Protocol, climate change was mentioned on average 0.45 times per report from 2001 to 2006. After 2006, average mentions increased to 1.7 times per report. Thus, although managers in the forest industry clearly responded to public opinion in increasing the treatment of climate change in annual reports after 2006, they did not feel the same urgency in dealing with the issue as did oil and gas executives.

In the cement industry, again as expected, there appears to be little relationship between public opinion and references to climate change in the annual reports of companies that participated in the study, although the trend is clearly up since 2000. Although references to climate change increased over the decade, there was no discernible change in 2007. Indeed, the largest increase in mentions of climate change took place in 2005, a year that means little to Canadians, but a lot to European business executives, since the European Unions Emissions Trading System came into effect on 1 January 2005, and would have been expected to receive considerable attention in that year's reports to shareholders for European companies.

Corporate annual reports thus demonstrate that, as expected, shifts in public opinion correlate not only with a shift in business preferences, but also with an observable increase in the treatment of climate change in reports to shareholders in the oil and gas and, to a lesser extent, forestry industries. This suggests that concern about investors' confidence did influence the change in business preferences for climate change policy instruments in Canada. In short, in these annual reports, the increased salience of the issue for the public appears to have been perceived as likely corresponding with its increased salience for shareholders. Indeed, the language used in relation to climate change in annual reports supports this analysis. Many companies, particularly in the oil and gas industry, listed climate change issues under the heading of "risks" or "risk management" (see, for example, ConocoPhillips Canada 2008; Encana 2008; Nexen 2008; Petro-Canada 2008; Suncor

Energy 2008). The subsequent texts then assured shareholders that, for that particular firm, the risks associated with climate change regulation were limited. For instance, in 2008 Nexen declared to shareholders: "We believe we are well positioned to meet the challenges of climate change and environmental regulations" (Nexen 2008). For these companies, assuring shareholders that they would continue to provide stable returns despite expected regulatory changes was a central objective of their communications on climate change.

Conclusion

The business community shifted its preference for climate change policy instruments en masse in 2006–07 because increased public attention to the issue changed expectations about the stability of the current regulatory regime, creating risk for the firms' capital investments' and highlighting a clear area of investors' concern. Public opinion per se about climate change did not cause the shift in firms' preferences, but it was a key indicator that the policy environment was changing and that investors were becoming concerned about investment risk in a carbon-constrained world. For business, therefore, attention to public opinion was not altruism or even merely a matter of finding favour with customers. As Avrim Lazar noted above, "the most critical factor in business success is attracting investment." Canadian business responded to the public opinion shift in 2006–07 by accepting the inevitability of carbon pricing and calling for that price to be implemented as soon as possible so as to re-establish regulatory equilibrium and provide certainty for investors.

Nothing in the change in public opinion or in firms' communications with shareholders, however, defined the type of carbon price that ought to be implemented. Instead, firms and industry associations were left to their own devices to determine which pricing mechanism – carbon taxation or cap-and-trade – they should support. How did they make this decision? If firms wished merely to choose the less costly of the two mechanisms, they would have overwhelmingly supported grandfathered cap-and-trade; in fact, firm's preferences were far less heterogeneous.

The risk-advantage model provides two explanations for firms' choices. First, firms will support a policy instrument that provides an advantage where possible. If they perceive no advantage, they will seek to limit the uncertainty related to future returns on investment – that is, risk – meaning that they will try not only to limit the absolute costs associated with compliance where possible, but also to ensure the predictability and stability of those costs. As these two requirements can lead to opposing preferences, decision-makers will tend to turn to previous experience with policy instruments to form their expectations about future effects. In the next two chapters, I examine these two arguments – advantage and experience – in turn.

Chapter Six

Advantage

The significance of competitive advantage to firms' decision-making is neither novel nor contested, but a fundamental concept in business strategy, well developed in the literature on the topic (Porter 1985). Accordingly, instead of redundantly establishing this connection, I present the findings of the interviews I conducted with representatives of firms and industry associations, highlighting the advantages that can flow from carbon-pricing mechanisms and how they influenced the policy preferences of participants in this study. In doing so, I hope to contribute to the environmental policy literature by stressing the complex ways in which policy instruments can influence market factors and, therefore, the competitiveness of particular products and firms over others.

The Forestry Industry: Direct Advantage

Firms can gain two types of advantage, direct and indirect, from a climate change policy instrument. A direct advantage is one that flows directly from the rules and regulations of the policy framework. The most obvious example is a firm's ability to sell allowances in a carbon market in a cap-and-trade program. Allowance sales not only reduce compliance costs, but also yield net profits to certain firms if the policy instrument is grandfathered and the firm is a net seller. This direct advantage led the forestry industry to act proactively on climate change far earlier than did other sectors and some firms and associations to view cap-and-trade in a positive light, despite the government intervention the policy implies.

In 2003 the Forest Products Association of Canada (FPAC) broke ranks with other business associations and signed a Memorandum of

Understanding with the federal government on the principles involved in a future cap-and-trade program. During that period, the FPAC led its members to pledge aggressive action to decrease greenhouse gas emissions to 57 per cent below 1990 levels by 2010 (FPAC 2010). In interviews, the association's leadership at the time remembered the displeasure that its active support of a regulatory instrument provoked among other industry associations, which saw the FPAC as being "on the other side of things" during this period, as Richard Hyndman of the Canadian Association of Petroleum Producers (CAPP) put it.

Why did the forestry industry association shift its climate change policy instrument preference three years before any other major association? The answer articulated by AbitibiBowater's manager of energy, development and strategy, Martin Fairbank, is hardly surprising:

> One of the main reasons that we have been progressive is that we do have the opportunity to use [low-emitting] waste biomass to replace fossil fuels. So, you cut the tree in the forest, you bring the logs to the sawmill, you take off the bark, and the bark is available right there, and it sort of gets a free ride because you don't charge any transportation costs for that bark from the forest to the sawmill, and if the sawmill is pretty close to the paper mill then the bark is almost free. Twenty years ago that bark was being buried because it was a lot easier to buy cheap oil and burn it in your boiler.

So waste biomass is available for consumption at the cost associated only with processing it, and it is very low in emissions compared with other fuel sources. Consequently, not only was the forestry industry better able to cut emissions than were other industries; it also could reduce costs by doing so. Still, although the fuel itself is almost free, the technological investment required to switch fuels is not. If firms were allowed to sell surplus emissions credits through a cap-and-trade program, however, they could offset most or all of this cost through the new revenue gained on the carbon market. Fairbank explained:

> It's also very expensive to build a boiler that's capable of burning a solid product like [biomass]. We just finished an investment that was $84 million at our St. Francis, Ontario, mill to build a biomass boiler, whereas you can buy a packaged natural gas boiler for maybe $10 million. Right now we are getting decent return on investment by the cost difference between natural gas and bark, provided we can keep the mill running all the time,

which is a problem right now. If there were carbon credits right now, it would be *really* a good investment.

Thus, the forestry industry's decision in 2003 to support cap-and-trade stemmed from the realization that the policy instrument provided considerable advantage to the industry, given the availability of a low-emitting and free alternative fuel source and the need to make considerable investments to exploit that fuel. Cap-and-trade would allow the industry to earn money by decreasing emissions and ensure an even greater return on investment in biomass boilers. Interestingly, however, the advantages became salient for decision-makers only after the risks of the policy were deemed negligible. Paul Lansbergen, the FPAC's director of energy, economics and climate change, argued: "I think [that], naturally, when it comes to government policy, everyone is going to assess the risks first. And in our case, the risks were much smaller and the opportunities much greater. So you look at the risks and [they are greater]; how do the rules really affect you on the ground? Given that and given our opportunities, how can we think of a different way of doing it such that it still meets the government's objective but positions us more on the opportunities side rather than [on] the risk side."

For most of the period after 2003, the policy instrument that positioned the forestry industry "more on the opportunities side" was cap-and-trade. Recently, however, some in the industry have become disillusioned by the federal government's continued movement of the base year on which allowances would be allocated. The 2003 Memorandum of Understanding promised the industry that, if it acted immediately, it would be credited for that action once an emissions-trading program was put in place. In 2008, however, the Harper government's "Turning the Corner" policy proposal set the base year for action at 2006, with little credit for earlier action. This left the industry "frustrated," according to the FPAC's Lansbergen, with the ever-changing details of a possible cap-and-trade program, particularly because the system would not reward much of its emission reductions.

By 2009 the FPAC no longer claimed to hold a specific preference for cap-and-trade versus carbon taxation. Under revenue-neutral carbon taxation, unlike cap-and-trade, firms would not be given a new revenue stream through credit sales, but they might receive cuts to corporate taxes while likely paying only minimal new taxes because of the industry's low emissions. Thus, if a later base year is assumed, the advantage of cap-and-trade decreases and firms begin to look at both policies, cap-and-trade and carbon tax, from the perspective of limiting risk. "The devil," FPAC president Avrim Lazar argued, "is in the details."

Nonetheless, while the FPAC's president claimed not to have a particular preference for cap-and-trade over taxation, Lansbergen stated that grandfathered cap-and-trade with offsets would be ideal for the industry; If the association could create the perfect instrument, it would be a specific form of emissions trading. Offsets are significant because they would allow forestry firms to gain revenue through sequestration activities and wood products manufacturers to sell credits, even though those operations likely would not be regulated in a cap-and-trade system. In addition, regulated industrial facilities, such as pulp and paper plants, would be in a good position to sell credits.

If grandfathered cap-and-trade with offsets would clearly provide advantage to the industry, why was the FPAC not strongly committed to the policy in 2009? Although the government's lack of support for early action certainly bred cynicism among industry executives, a second explanation – which I explore in Chapter 6 – for the association's hesitancy is the lack of consensus in the industry. For some forestry firms headquartered in British Columbia, for example, the certain, status quo option was a carbon tax, reflecting a changed risk assessment of cap-and-trade versus carbon taxation for those firms. The BC firms that participated in the study clearly were not enamoured with a carbon tax, but they were surprisingly reticent to argue against it. Firms outside of the province, however, remained committed to cap-and-trade.

Natural Gas and the Railways: Indirect Advantage

Indirect advantage can accrue to a firm from the influence that a climate change policy instrument might have on a third party – generally, the firm's customers. If the firm expects a particular policy instrument to offer an incentive to customers to purchase its product (relative to an alternative), it will prefer that policy instrument. Interestingly, however, the type of policy instrument the firm will prefer tends to depend on the type of market on which the firm is currently focused or wishes to expand into, and on the emissions intensity of alternative products in a given jurisdiction.

The two natural gas firms that participated in the study were strongly in favour of a carbon tax, and invoked three arguments to support this preference. First, both Union Gas president Julie Dill and Encana executive vice president Gerry Protti believed that a tax would support the current choices of individual consumers, their main clients in the residential heating market. Second, they thought that a tax would open up a new market by giving electric utilities a clear incentive to switch from higher-emitting coal to lower-emitting natural gas; quite simply, a carbon tax would make coal relatively more expensive and natural gas relatively less expensive to the utility. A third possibility, highlighted by Protti, was that natural gas could serve as the fuel of choice for the North American transportation fleet, provided that a price incentive would cause political demand for an expansion of the required infrastructure.

The first argument is straightforward, and refers to the issue of the scope of a policy instrument. Carbon taxation would directly and visibly charge both residential and corporate customers of fossil fuel firms for the emissions in the product, while cap-and-trade almost always limits inclusion in the program to large final emitters. With a carbon tax, current residential clients of natural gas firms would have one more reason to be thankful for their choice of energy source, while residents using other fuels (in Ontario, primarily oil or electricity generated from coal) would be given an incentive to switch.

In the traditional large emitter cap-and-trade program, however, this market would be unlikely to be covered by the cap, so natural gas firms would not have a price advantage over other fuel alternatives in the residential sector. It is possible that cap-and-trade would force fuel producers, suppliers, transporters, or distributors to hold credits to cover the carbon content in the product, creating a system that would cover both residential and large-scale clients, but this type of policy instrument design has not been the focus of previous Canadian government policy debates. Since natural gas is now the fuel of choice in the residential markets in both Alberta and Ontario, the two firms in the study appeared *certain* that a carbon tax would only support that position, while simultaneously providing opportunities for expansion where possible. From the firms' perspective, however, cap-and-trade provided no such certainty: as Union Gas's Dill put it, "I have no idea how a cap-and-trade system is going to impact a residential customer of Union Gas."

The second argument – that utilities might switch to natural gas after the implementation of a carbon tax – highlights the weighing of risks and advantages in a firm's analysis of policy instruments. As Encana's Gerri Protti explained:

One of the messages that we've been giving to governments is that you are underplaying the role that natural gas can play in the North American economy. For example, did you know that there is more installed nameplate generating capacity for natural gas in the US, by far, than coal? Everyone talks about coal. The amount of energy produced by coal is [gestures above head], the amount of energy produced by natural gas is [gestures chest high], [the] capacity [of natural gas] is [gestures above head] versus [coal, gestures low]. The reason is that [coal capacity is] base load, [natural gas capacity] is peaking units, ... and utilities have had a systemic bias for coal. They're often integrated with coal companies, and that's the base load, and that's what they understand. You could have an immediate environmental impact by just taking those [natural gas] units and burning them more. Now, you're probably going to pay more, even at these lower prices, for the natural gas than for the coal, so the electricity price would go up and, the utilities – that's just not something they're interested in.

From the perspective of executives at both natural gas firms in the study, as Protti put it, "once again [this] leads you to a carbon tax." In other words, carbon taxation would clearly and simply increase the cost of coal to utilities relative to that of natural gas and, it was thought, increase the likelihood of their using natural gas. Theoretically, the type of large cap-and-trade program for large emitters discussed in Canada should have the same effect, since this argument relates to changes in behaviour by large final emitters – namely, the electrical utilities. Forcing utilities to buy credits for emissions should cause coal to be relatively more expensive and natural gas to be relatively less expensive to the utility. Interestingly, however, both Dill and Protti were unconvinced of this effect, strongly preferring a carbon tax. Indeed, when asked why cap-and-trade would not also increase the cost of coal to utilities, Dill responded that it would not, "because [they] can just buy credits."

The response might indicate a misunderstanding on the part of the interview subject about the working of cap-and-trade – after all, it is by forcing firms to buy credits that cap-and-trade would increase the price of coal. However, the rest of the discussion suggests that, actually, natural gas executives had a strong understanding of the risk-advantage implications of both policy instruments to their industry, and that this understanding determined their preferences for carbon taxation. Both executives held the view that the many options available in the details of a cap-and-trade system create risk and uncertainty, whereas the simplicity of carbon taxation creates only advantage, since it not only would support their firms' position in the residential market; it clearly and efficiently would also increase the cost of coal to utilities. The two executives highlighted the potential for "gamesmanship" among speculators and market actors, as well as possible loopholes in the regulations themselves – including subsidies or unfair allowances to certain industries, such as coal – to reduce the effect of price increases on utilities under cap-and-trade. As Protti explained,

> [carbon taxation provides] an efficient vehicle for pricing. So, if you have a choice, say, [with a carbon tax] "here is your cost, go away and do what you need to do to minimize it" versus [with cap-and-trade] "here's a set of legislation, we're going to put regulations to it but we're not exactly sure how we're going to do it," we have to determine what facilities are going to be eligible, what exemptions there might be, and it gets really complex. What that introduces for an executive team of a company and for the board of directors is risk, because you can't quantify it.

Thus, two issues interact to create a clear preference for carbon taxation by these firms. First, the scope of a carbon tax as affecting both residential and commercial customers means that the policy instrument would provide an advantage in all areas of the economy in which natural gas firms either currently operate or hope to expand, including the residential heating market, the transportation market, and the electricity market. Cap-and-trade would directly, and therefore with certainty, cover only the electricity market. It could conceivably cover the other two markets, but that would depend on the details of the policy instrument, and the extent of the impact would be difficult to determine in advance.

The second issue is that, even in the electricity sector, the uncertainty surrounding emissions-trading regulations for natural gas and the possibility of gamesmanship create a perception of risk for natural gas firms, while carbon taxation, given its clarity and simplicity, creates only a perception of advantage. In other words, executives have complete faith that a carbon tax would affect their markets as they expect, creating a clear advantage for their product, but lack that faith with respect to cap-and-trade.

To some extent, this level of uncertainty concerning cap-and-trade is indicative of the particular nature of the natural gas industry. In a 2008 report to the US Congress on cap-and-trade, the Pew Center on Global Climate Change (2008) highlighted the natural gas industry as a particularly complex industry to regulate through cap-and-trade for a number of reasons: it includes large and small emitters, generates fugitive methane emissions throughout the supply chain, changes hands multiple times between production and the end user, and can also be incorporated into manufactured products without combustion (and, thus, emission). Policy-makers, therefore, would have to examine many options in developing a cap-and-trade program to deal with this industry, making it impossible for firms to know the details before the program is developed. To avoid this complexity and to optimize advantage, the overwhelming favourite of these firms is a carbon tax.

In Quebec, however, where Gaz Métro supported cap-and-trade, none of these advantages would apply, for a couple of reasons. First, the alternative fuel for the public utility in that province is not higher-emitting coal, but zero-emitting hydro, so neither a carbon tax nor cap-and-trade would offer an incentive to increase the use of natural gas in Quebec's electricity sector. Second, Gaz Métro is not a significant player in the residential heating and cooking sector in Quebec, where 78 per cent of residential space heating is fueled by lower-emitting electricity and wood. Consequently, a carbon tax would neither increase the attractiveness of natural gas as a fuel source in relation to the alternative in the market, nor would its scope and effect on residents matter to Gaz Métro. Unlike those of the other natural gas firms in this study, the majority of Gaz Métro's customers are large-emitting commercial firms. A former Gaz Métro official I interviewed said that, as both a carbon tax and traditional cap-and-trade would cover large emitters directly, the firm compared the effect of each policy and decided that cap-and-trade would provide greater flexibility for its customers. This decision, however, was not about supporting a policy instrument that provided a clear advantage for fuel switching, but about choosing between the lesser of two evils: the least risky policy.

The Railway Association of Canada (RAC), on the other hand, supported cap-and-trade for a similar reason that the Alberta and Ontario natural gas firms supported a carbon tax: it believed the policy instrument would provide an incentive for its main customers – commercial shippers – to switch from trucking to railways. RAC president Cliff MacKay explained the difference in perspective between Ontario and Alberta's natural gas companies and his association:

[They want carbon taxation] because their major customers are consumers. Our major customers are corporate shippers. So, for us, a 3 per cent at the margin change in price as a result of a cap-and-trade system [would really matter to our commercial customers] or our being able to say to Dow Chemical, "we can give you an advantage if you use rail because we can then pass our credits on to you." It makes a difference. It makes no difference to the average consumer. You'd have to have a 10, 15, 20 per cent hit [for the consumer to actually change].

Consequently, since railways are lower emitters than the alternative land-based shipping form – trucking – they would have an advantage in a low-carbon economy. Moreover, unlike the natural gas firms above, the railway industry's overwhelming focus on commercial clients makes cap-and-trade an appropriate policy instrument to cause the behavioural change it seeks – namely, a switch to rail.

Interestingly, advantages also influence an industry's competitiveness as an investment vehicle, as RAC president MacKay explained:

From the shareholder side ... I would call it interest. Shareholders and analysts see our environmental advantages as perhaps being a contributor to shareholder value over time, as life unfolds. It's one of the factors that leads a lot of analysts to say openly that, notwithstanding the short-term stuff we're living through at the moment, rail has a fairly bright long-term growth future. It's not the only issue but it's one of the issues. So, from a shareholder/investor view, environment tends to be a positive for us as opposed to a negative. It's a different kind of game.

Thus, for the railways, not only would cap-and-trade offer the possibility of increased demand, and therefore revenue; it also would assuage investors' concerns and strengthen the industry's investment status, despite some recent financial problems.[11]

Conclusion

In previous chapters I explained why a firm might prefer a regulatory policy instrument to a less costly voluntary initiative. In this chapter, I began to explain how a firm might choose one regulatory policy

---

11 Even if the perception and *reality* of risk related to rail safety have increased since the Lac Mégantic disaster.

instrument over another. A direct advantage, which flows directly from the policy instrument itself, would give firms opportunities to expand their market share and revenue stream. An indirect advantage could create the same opportunities, but as a result of the policy instrument's effect on the incentives and costs faced by the firm's customers – or potential customers.

Interestingly, advantages appear to influence firms and associations in a relatively predictable manner: if a particular policy instrument provided such advantages, firms and associations strongly supported it. The only exception was the forestry industry, whose association was more hesitant to support grandfathered cap-and-trade than expected. In most cases, however, firms whose products were lower emitting than alternatives supported the policy instrument whose scope would directly cover their customers in key markets, either commercial or residential.

Climate change policy instruments do not offer a competitive advantage to all firms and, therefore, not all firms can base their policy instrument preferences on analyses of advantage. I now turn to the second manner in which firms choose policy instruments: by seeking to limit the risk associated with a regulatory change and, in this regard, it is previous experience that provides the key to understanding business preferences for particular carbon-pricing mechanisms.

Chapter Seven

Experience

When it comes to business preferences for climate change policy instruments, a firm's previous experience with an instrument matters significantly. With previous experience, a firm's executives can see for themselves the instrument's effects on the returns on the firm's capital investments and on its ability to compete for capital. In other words, experience acts as a heuristic device: if executives assume that an instrument's future effects on the firm will be similar to those of the past, they will develop a degree of certainty over the effects of the instrument, which will lower the perception of risk to the firm. Indeed, a clear correlation exists between previous experience and current support for an instrument. Thus, the variation in support of particular carbon-pricing instruments – some firms and associations support cap-and-trade, others support carbon taxation, and still others have no preference – is largely explained by the fact that some firms would receive advantage from certain instruments while other would not *and* by firms' previous experience with particular instrument. These two variables – advantage and experience – taken together explain the variation in carbon-pricing preferences observed in this study. Before delving into this evidence, however, it is important to put this analysis in context; I begin by discussing how preferences based on lower perceived risk differ from those based on advantage and why not all the observed variation can be explained by differences in perceived advantage.

Limiting Risk: Examples and Variation

One of the most puzzling empirical observations in this study is that firms in the same industry and with similar product mixes and corporate circumstances adopted completely different preferences for carbon-pricing mechanisms. Evidence suggests that, although the influence of advantages on policy instrument preferences tends to be relatively uniform across firms facing similar corporate circumstances and market factors, there is considerable variation in the preferences of firms without an apparent competitive advantage, and no clear market factor adequately explains this variation. Although a clear perception of advantage explains support for carbon taxation by two firms in the study and for cap-and-trade by another three, the majority of firms' carbon-pricing preferences remain to be explained. As already discussed, this variation cannot be explained by a simple cost analysis (fewer than half the firms in the study supported grandfathered cap-and-trade despite the lower cost it would entail). How, then, do firms facing only risk from a policy instrument determine their preferences?

The risk-advantage model provides an explanation both for the existence of variation in policy instrument preferences among similar firms and for the type of instrument firms ultimately chose to support. Firms, seeking to decrease the risk associated with the regulatory realm, would like to keep compliance costs low and to ensure cost predictability and stability over the long term, but these two requirements can provide contradictory logic vis-à-vis carbon-pricing instruments. On the one hand, a grandfathered cap-and-trade program typically is considerably cheaper than a carbon tax, but the market-determined price and the existence of complex program designs make predicting the exact price and overall cost difficult. On the other hand, once government sets a tax rate, carbon taxation provides far more price predictability than a market-determined carbon price. Yet, since a grandfathered cap-and-trade program would be paid only on emissions over a set quota and the exact cost would depend on the amount of other tax returned under revenue neutrality, a carbon tax would offer neither complete cost predictability nor the most likely lowest-cost option (see Chapter 1). In short, firms that like carbon pricing because of its regulatory stability but that do not perceive an advantage in either option, have a difficult choice to make: which pricing instrument would have the *least* negative effect on the firm?

In some cases, the executives I interviewed were able to construct a logical explanation of why one carbon-pricing instrument was "less bad" than the other. The perspective of the Canadian Petroleum Products Institute (CPPI), which represented petroleum refiners – it changed its name to the Canadian Fuels Association in 2012 – provides a good example of an association aiming to mitigate the risk associated with a public policy instrument. Although the CPPI did not have an official preference for a climate change policy instrument, the representative suggested that a carbon tax had considerable "traction" within the industry because the price on the product's emissions would be paid, not by the refiner, but by the consumer, preventing US refineries from gaining an unfair advantage. The CPPI was concerned that the refining industry would relocate to the United States if Canadian refiners faced a price on carbon under cap-and-trade while US refiners did not. Absent border adjustments – which the representative appeared sceptical would be put in place, given trade agreements – cheaper gasoline from the United States might then enter the Canadian market, while more expensive Canadian gasoline might become uncompetitive in the US market. A carbon tax, on the other hand, would be paid at the point of sale, meaning that all gasoline sold in Canada would be treated equally, whether refined in the United States or in Canada. This would avoid any need for complicated tariffs or border adjustments. Although CPPI representative Tony Macerollo acknowledged that a cap-and-trade system could provide the same security, depending on the point of regulation, he appeared to view carbon taxation as assuaging competitiveness concerns with greater simplicity and certainty. The only possible downside would be a decline in revenue should the carbon tax lower demand. The representative appeared confident, however, that Canadian consumers would be willing to pay fairly high prices for gasoline before they started changing their behaviour.

Perhaps the most interesting aspect of the explanation of the CPPI's perspective is not its interest in a carbon tax, but the fact that the institute was unable to form a clear preference based on this analysis. Despite the strong logic in favour of taxation for refiners, the institute faced considerable variation in preference among its member firms. Indeed, in the Canadian petroleum industry more broadly, there was significant variation in preferences in 2009. Some firms supported carbon taxation (Nexen, ConocoPhillips Canada), while others support cap-and-trade (Shell Canada, ConocoPhillips in the United States, Suncor Energy).

The most obvious explanation for lack of agreement among refiners is that the modern multinational corporation is a maze of horizontal and vertical integration, which means that one corporate banner could fly over a number of products and processes. Different products could imply different preference logics. Consequently, firms and associations might face choosing between a policy instrument that is a source of less risk in one area of operations but high risk in another area, and a policy instrument with the opposite problem. This is equally the case for advantages. Indeed, attempting to prevent this sort of contradictory logic of risk and advantage was part of the reason Encana chose to split its oil and natural gas operations into two separate companies. Encana now focuses solely on natural gas, while Cenovus, created in 2009, took over petroleum operations (at the time of the interview, they remained one corporation, but the split was already planned). Senior Encana executive Gerri Protti explained:

> One of the reasons for doing that is that the people who work the oil projects have a different set of issues than the people that work in natural gas projects, also a different set of opportunities. We're going to need both hydrocarbons. [Natural gas] is dramatically different in terms of the carbon load of a unit of energy ... and people think that's the only thing [that is going to matter]. Natural gas also has no particulates, no mercury. Things like coal and oil have ... So the fact [is that] natural gas and oil in our company are competing against one another [and, we believe,] they are not really competing as much as they should be.

Yet multiple products in one company do not appear to explain all of the variation in carbon-pricing preferences. Many companies with similar product mixes supported different instruments – Suncor Energy and Shell Canada for cap-and-trade, ConocoPhillips Canada and Nexen for a carbon tax, for instance. In the cement industry, where the product and processes tend to be homogeneous, Essroc was strongly against cap-and-trade despite the rest of the industry's unanimous support for that policy instrument. Although executives at these companies tended to use the same sort of arguments in favour of their preferred policy instrument – cap-and-trade is cheaper and more flexible, while taxation offers greater price predictability and simplicity – the arguments themselves do not explain the variation but instead merely reframe the puzzle: why are certain arguments in favour of certain instruments more compelling for some firms than others? Why do some firms prefer the lower costs associated with a grandfathered cap-and-trade program while others prefer the higher price predictability of a carbon tax?

Interview subjects highlighted a possible answer to this question: firms are more likely to support a policy instrument with which they have previous experience. I argue that experience allows firms to judge policy instruments for themselves, instead of basing their preferences on theoretical arguments or expert advice. Furthermore, experience gives firms perceived certainty about the effects of a policy instrument, which in most cases lowers the perception of risk. Although theoretical arguments can be contradictory, creating doubts about their validity, experience is viewed as undeniable. This is the familiarity effect.[12]

The Familiarity Effect

Interview subjects often referred to previous experience in explaining their firm's or association's preference. Among European-owned firms, the European Union Emissions Trading System (EU ETS) generally increased support for cap-and-trade. The representative from Shell Canada, for instance, argued: "Shell has been instrumental and very closely engaged in the development of the EU ETS. And so I think it is natural that we would have a much higher comfort level with a cap-and-trade system, but – at the same time – we are dealing in new territory [with a carbon tax]. There has never been a carbon tax that has been applied as broadly as it would have to be if we were going to implement it ... There isn't a lot of experience out there and what there is is on cap-and-trade." Interestingly, although the European system's price volatility was sometimes cited as a reason *not* to support cap-and-trade, firms with considerable experience with it never made this argument. Holcim Canada's Luc Robitalle, for instance, referred to the problems, but still viewed this experience as positive and part of the firm's support for cap-and-trade. What appeared important was that, with cap-and-trade, the firm knew where the pitfalls lay: "It's great that the EU ETS is in place because it allows us to see what works and what doesn't work. For example, we realize now how important the baseline information is when you come up with the target and how having the policies improperly done can affect competitiveness."

The sulphur oxides (SO_x) and nitrogen oxides (NO_x) emissions-trading program in the United States also gave firms an opportunity to experience cap-and-trade. For an official at Weyerhaeuser, this was

---

12 As discussed in Chapter 1, I assume that multiple people engage in a firm's decision-making and, therefore, that the firm itself must have experienced the instrument for it to have an effect. I do not assume learning between firms occurs when managers move, even though some managers might be familiar with a policy instrument from their experience at another firm.

integral to the company's preference: "We did sell some emission credits and we thought it was a really good program ... I'm not sure if it was
our company's success or the overall success of the program." Robert
Page, chair of the National Round Table on the Environment and the
Economy (NRTEE), said that experience with sulphur dioxide offsets
also drove his former company, TransAlta, in its policy preference, as
executives learned that the utility could make money through emissions trading. According to Page,

> when it actually happened that we got three times the price for those SO_2
> credits than I'd estimated ... this made a real difference to the Board's
> assessment even on my conservative estimates. Then, when it turned out
> that we made even more than that and that [emissions trading] was a sig-
> nificant way of financing our new technology investment in those plants ...
> the company then came to understand that I, with all the emission credits
> that I sold and all the wind power that I brought to the company, became a
> profit centre for the company.

Interview subjects were clear that experience matters to firms, but
why does it matter? The question is important because the evidence
required to support the argument, independent of the perceptions of
interview subjects, depends on the causal mechanism at work. Experience could influence business preferences for climate change policy
instruments in two ways. First, a firm with previous experience with an
instrument would be expected to have the processes and expertise in
place to handle that program's administrative requirements efficiently
and at less cost than alternatives, thus influencing the firm's support of
the future use of that instrument over others. This is merely a reframing
of the cost-benefit arguments so pervasive in the literature.

Second, direct experience with a particular instrument might give
managers a greater sense of certainty about its effects and a way to differentiate between competing logics in favour of each instrument. In
other words, when decision-makers are familiar with a policy instrument and its effects on the firm, they are more likely to feel comfortable
with it and to assume that previous experience predicts the design and
effects of a future program. A known problem is generally perceived as
better than the uncertainty associated with the unknown – unless, of
course, the previous experience was one of significant damage to the
firm. If the damage was associated with a particular detail that could
be avoided or was not an integral aspect of the instrument, however,

decision-makers might still prefer the previously experienced instrument over others. This argument stems directly from the risk-advantage model.

Robert Page, in explaining his personal preference as chair of the NRTEE , summed up this reasoning succinctly: "My personal preference is for a cap-and-trade system because I've seen it work. I understand it. It gives companies an option to be entrepreneurial. To find the least cost options. Not to just sit back and take a tax between the eyes. There is no business judgment that's involved with the carbon tax. So I tend to prefer a cap-and-trade system over just a straight carbon tax ... I guess a fall back on what I understand and what I've done." Howlett and Ramesh (2005) make a similar argument in relation to the choice of policy instrument by *government*: policy-makers are more likely to favour instruments with which they have previous experience because it allows them instinctively to employ objective and rational decision-making. Otherwise, the number of unknowns prevents such analyses, leaving policy-makers to guess at outcomes without a point of reference.

Demonstrating the significance of experience on firms' policy preferences, therefore, requires the observation of two correlations. First, if experience indeed matters, there should be a clear relationship between a firm's previous experience and its declared preference. Second, if the perception of certainty gained from managerial familiarity is what drives the link between experience and preference, then the location of that experience – near to the offices of the preference decision-makers – would be significant. Managers must have a level of connection and personal experience with the policy instrument for familiarity to have an effect. If cost efficiencies are the driving force, however, it should not matter where the experience was gained.

The first of the two correlations is clear among the firms in this study. Six of the ten firms[13] with experience only of cap-and-trade supported that system, with representatives of those firms directly citing their experience as a reason for their preference. When I removed from the sample those firms with only peripheral experience of cap-and-trade – in a jurisdiction on a different continent than the company's

---

13 Firms with experience of the Alberta system are not included in this count because that system is a hybrid that does not fit the traditional conceptualization of either cap-and-trade or a carbon tax, and therefore is excluded from the analysis.

head office – the correlation between experience and preference increased to six of eight firms and, of the remaining two, one cited unofficial support for cap-and-trade. Experience of a carbon tax also decreased support for cap-and-trade among forestry firms despite the advantage the latter would offer the industry.

Representatives of seven firms – Suncor Energy, TransAlta,[14] Abiti-biBowater, Weyerhaeuser, Shell Canada, Holcim Canada, and Lehigh – pointed directly to their firm's positive experience with cap-and-trade as significant for its support of the policy instrument. Suncor Energy was an early pioneer in emissions trading, having taken part in the first post-Kyoto cross-border trade in 1997 with Niagara Mohawk Power in the United States. The trade, facilitated by Environmental Defense Fund, a US-based non-governmental organization, was a success, according to Suncor's Gordon Lambert, prompting the company to commit to cap-and-trade thereafter. Interestingly, although Lehigh's representative cited past experience as a reason for the firm's unofficial preference, the firm had no official preference for either carbon-pricing instrument. TransAlta, AbitibiBowater, and Weyerhaeuser all had experience with the US SO_x and NO_x cap-and-trade program, which they viewed favourably. Shell Canada, Holcim Canada, and Lehigh Cement, as European-owned companies, had experience with the EU ETS, which became operational in 2005. In every case, the firm's previous experience with cap-and-trade was cited as a significant reason why it now supported the policy instrument.

In the previous chapter I demonstrated that a firm was likely to support any policy instrument from which it would gain a clear advantage. I should note, therefore, that, among the above firms, only AbitibiBowater and Weyerhaeuser, two forestry firms, also would receive a clear market advantage from grandfathered cap-and-trade. For these two firms, there was a double incentive to support cap-and-trade; consequently, it is impossible to determine which influence was stronger using qualitative methodology.

---

14 Evidence on TransAlta's preferences and experience was provided by Robert Page, former vice president of sustainability for the corporation. I excluded TransAlta from most of the analysis of preferences in the previous chapters because Mr Page was no longer affiliated with TransAlta at the time of the interview and TransAlta was not, strictly speaking, a "participating firm." Here, however, only the firm's experience and preference, both of which are available from the interview data, need to be known. TransAlta is also not included in the summary in Chapter 1, which explains the slight discrepancy in figures.

The other firms, however, were developing preferences in the absence of a clear advantage, and would be expected to have focused instead on limiting risk. For these firms, previous experience appears to have decreased the perception of risk associated with the policy instrument.

Interestingly, the only firms in the study to have direct experience with carbon taxation also appeared to be influenced by this experience, in this case by counteracting the effect of the clear advantage of cap-and-trade. Forestry companies would be expected to benefit the most from a grandfathered cap-and-trade program because of the industry's ability to lower emissions cost-effectively. Nonetheless, the three forestry firms in the study that were operating in British Columbia did not have a clear official preference for that instrument. Each was hesitant to declare a preference at all, although Canfor's Mike Bradley and Catalyst Paper's Lyn Brown stated personal preferences: the former for cap-and-trade and the latter for a carbon tax.

Given the clear advantage of cap-and-trade to the forestry industry, this lack of official preference on the part of these BC firms is surprising. It also stands in stark contrast to the clear official preferences of the two forestry firms headquartered outside British Columbia (AbitibiBowater and Weyerhaeuser), both of which strongly supported cap-and-trade as expected. Although none of the BC companies appeared completely enamoured with carbon taxation, each referred to the simplicity of the system and suggested that there were pros and cons to both cap-and-trade and carbon taxation. It should be noted that none of the BC firms had experience with cap-and-trade, unlike AbitibiBowater and Weyerhaeuser. Ultimately, experience with a revenue-neutral carbon tax appears to have prevented BC firms from dismissing the policy option altogether and to have enhanced their perceptions of the positive aspects of taxation, which otherwise might have been ignored.[15] In other words, experience appears to be a more significant influence

---

15 It could be argued that BC firms were less supportive of cap-and-trade, not because of their experience with carbon taxation, but because they hoped to see policy convergence across jurisdictions, so that they would have to face only one policy instrument, not different ones in different jurisdictions. Nothing that the interview subjects said, however, suggested this factor. Indeed, the one interviewee who referred to policy convergence did so as a reason not to support taxation, believing that cap-and-trade was the most likely instrument to be adopted nationally and internationally. It should be recalled that Stéphane Dion's electoral loss related to his carbon tax policy the previous year had made carbon taxation a political hot potato federally.

on preferences than advantage. If, as noted, for Avrim Lazar of the Forest Products Association of Canada, "the devil is in the details," it also appears that business officials preferred *the devil they knew.*

This is not to say that, in all cases, experience increases a positive association with an instrument. Essroc pointed to its negative experience with the US SO_x and NO_x cap-and-trade program as the main reason the company was firmly against the policy instrument. Its representative, Gary Molchan, stated that the company was particularly concerned about speculation, and saw the instrument as controlled by "bandits in the woods": the bankers and brokers who would take a cut of each transaction. Instead, if carbon pricing were inevitable, the company preferred taxation. Interestingly, this is the only case in which prior experience was cited as the reason for *not* supporting a policy instrument.

There are two outliers in this pattern of experiential influence on risk assessments. Nexen and ConocoPhillips Canada, although both supporting a carbon tax in Canada, had some experience with emissions trading in their UK operations. Unlike other firms with previous experience with a carbon tax in their home country, however, theirs was limited to a peripheral region of operations well removed from their head offices in western North America.

These outliers thus support an underlying assumption of the analysis – namely, that managerial familiarity with a policy instrument leads to an increased perception of certainty, and that it is this certainty that matters, rather than increased efficiency through harmonized policies across the firm. At first glance, it might appear that experience matters because of the increased efficiencies associated with harmonized policy. Already having the administrative processes in place to deal with a particular policy instrument, a firm might believe it cheaper to support that policy than to gear up for another. There is undoubtedly some truth to this: if the only reason for the correlation was that previous experience could be expected to lead to increased efficiency and lower costs, then the location of the experience should have had little effect. ConocoPhillips, for instance, could transplant its institutional knowledge and expertise from its UK experience to Canada (interview subjects referred to prior circumstances in which personnel with climate change expertise were transferred from one arm of the company to another to augment the knowledge base).

Instead, I argue that experience is significant in the development of a firm's preference of policy instrument because it offers the perception of certainty over outcome. Managers who have personally experienced the effects of a policy instrument and seen the firm survive will assume that future experience with the policy instrument will mirror past experience. Its effects are known and viewed as more certain, and the instrument is therefore seen as a lesser risk to the firm, making objective investment choices more possible. This perception, however, requires that decision-makers be comfortable and familiar with the policy instrument (otherwise, it remains an unknown). That perception would be strongest when the experience is in the jurisdiction in which the firm's decision-makers are based and weakest when it is many jurisdictions removed from those offices.

As Table 2 illustrates, the findings support this interpretation: Of the thirteen firms with previous experience with an instrument, only four

Table 2. Carbon-pricing Instruments: Experience, Advantage, and Preferences of Selected Firms, Canada, 2009

Firm	Previous Experience	Apparent Advantage	Preference
In Same Jurisdiction as Head Office			
Suncor Energy	Cap-and-trade		Cap-and-trade
AbitibiBowater	Cap-and-trade	Cap-and-trade	Cap-and-trade
Weyerhaeuser	Cap-and-trade	Cap-and-trade	Cap-and-trade
Shell Canada	Cap-and-trade		Cap-and-trade
Holcim Canada	Cap-and-trade		Cap-and-trade
Lehigh Cement	Cap-and-trade		No preference
TransAlta	Cap-and-trade		Cap-and-trade
Essroc	Cap-and-trade		Voluntary or carbon tax
Canfor	Carbon tax	Cap-and-trade	No preference
West Fraser Timber	Carbon tax	Cap-and-trade	No preference
Catalyst Paper	Carbon tax	Cap-and-trade	No preference
Outside Head Office Jurisdiction			
Nexen	Cap-and-trade (UK – head office in Calgary)		Carbon tax
ConocoPhillips Canada	Cap-and-trade (UK – head office in Calgary/ Houston)		Carbon tax
No Experience			
St. Mary's Cement	No	Cap-and-trade	Cap-and-trade
Union Gas	No	Carbon tax	Carbon tax
Encana	No	Carbon tax	Carbon tax
Petro-Canada	No	No	No preference
Gaz Métro	No	No	Cap-and-trade

Note: Lehigh had no official preference despite its past experience, but its representative declared strong support for cap-and-trade.
Source: Author's compilation.

did not appear positively influenced by that experience. Of those, two firms had only peripheral experience with the policy. In all of the nine cases in which there was a positive correlation between experience and support, past experience was in the same continent, and generally in same jurisdiction, as the head office where key decision-makers were based.

Conclusion

Almost all the firms that participated in this study articulated support for carbon pricing in general, but they could not agree on which type of carbon-pricing instrument ought to be implemented. Eight firms supported cap-and-trade, five supported carbon taxation, and five had no preference. Although their representatives often made similar arguments in support of their preference – cap-and-trade is cheaper and more flexible; taxation provides greater price predictability, efficiency, and simplicity – it was not immediately clear why some firms dismissed arguments that others found compelling; these arguments could not, in themselves, explain the variation in policy instrument preferences among firms. When previous experience and perceived advantage are examined in relation to preferences, as in Table 2, however, patterns begin to emerge:

1. If a firm had previous experience with a carbon-pricing instrument in the same jurisdiction as its head office (local experience), but would gain no apparent advantage from either cap-and-trade or a carbon tax, it supported the instrument with which it had experience.
2. If a firm had local experience with an instrument and could expect to receive an advantage from its future implementation, the firm supported that instrument.
3. If a firm had local experience with one instrument, but could expect to receive advantage from another, it had no official preference.
4. If a firm had no local experience with a policy instrument, it supported the instrument from which it expected to gain advantage.
5. If a firm had no local experience with an instrument and could expect no advantage from one, the reason for its choice of instrument was not apparent – indeed, the preference was somewhat random, with two in favour of a carbon tax, one with no preference, and one in favour of cap-and-trade.

The only two outliers in this pattern of preference were Essroc, which opposed cap-and-trade despite its experience in both the United States and Europe, and Lehigh, which, despite its experience with cap-and-trade in Europe, had no official preference.

The most significant predictor of firms' preferences was decision-makers' familiarity with a policy instrument through past experience, even above the clear advantage a firm might gain from another instrument. Experience matters, since it increases the perceived certainty of outcome and, thus, affects corporate decision-makers' evaluation of the risk the instrument entails.

In the preceding four chapters, I demonstrated the utility of the risk-advantage model in explaining, first, the 2006–07 shift in aggregate business preferences for carbon-pricing instruments and, second, the variation in preferences between firms in 2009. To this end, the model provides considerable benefit by shifting the focus away from the cost of an instrument to other significant variables that affect the success of a firm – particularly expectations of the impact of different policies, third-party investors' concerns, the advantage accruing from a particular instrument, and previous experience with it. Changing expectations of future policy instrument implementation and the resulting increase in perceived investors' concerns led to a general shift in industry preference in favour of carbon pricing in 2006–07. Variation in the type of carbon price firms subsequently supported can be explained either by the advantages offered by a particular policy instrument or by firms' experience with it – a variable that significantly affects assessments of risk. As such, the risk-advantage model provides a good foundation for understanding corporate preferences for climate change policy instruments in Canada.

Chapter Eight

The Ideas of Managers: A Null Finding with Potential

Interview subjects often referred to the convictions or beliefs of key decision-makers as significant in determining business preferences for climate change policy instruments. Representatives told stories about their leaders and how their personal convictions had influenced the company. Unfortunately, I found no independent evidence to support this claim. Indeed, it appears that leaders' convictions had limited, if any, effect on a firm's preferences independent of the familiarity effect. This does not mean that the ideas of key managers are of no import: their perceptions of risk – as relating to short-term or long-term expected profits – might affect a firm's broader actions on the environment, a finding that, while preliminary, suggests a significant avenue for future research.

Convictions and Beliefs

In the first phase of my research, interview subjects highlighted the convictions or beliefs of key decision-makers in determining firms' preferences of climate change policy instrument. For instance, a former Petro-Canada official, in explaining the firm's hesitance to announce a climate change policy preference, stated: "I'd say the [chief executive officer] sets the tone for sure." The interviewer clarified, "So, another CEO may have gone another direction?" Response: "Absolutely." Other interview subjects – for example, Julie Dill of Union Gas and Bob Mitchell of ConocoPhillips Canada – also referred to the significance of their CEO in supporting a particular preference, often telling stories about the CEO's personal or professional history or even family situation. Clearly, interview subjects believed that the values leaders brought to their firm had a significant impact on its policy instrument preference.

This was equally true of associations as of firms. Canfor's Mike Bradley, previously chair of the climate change committee of the Forest Products Association of Canada (FPAC), described how the association's staff influenced firms in supporting emissions trading in 2003: "Someone's got to convince [the CEOs] that there might be more to gain by doing this than lost. And that's where groups like FPAC played a very important role ... If you'd had a different group there, they could have actually argued against it. They could have all these compelling reasons why not to do it ... the leadership of the group [makes the difference]. That's the people – they're personalities, where their hearts are."

Although interview subjects clearly viewed convictions and beliefs of particular individuals as important, testing the significance of these variables in the second phase of research presented a particular methodological challenge. If personal convictions and beliefs were a significant determinant of policy instrument preferences, one would expect evidence of a pattern of preference change when and if the firm's or association's leadership changes. Uncovering such a pattern, however, requires knowledge about the internal workings of a firm or association, an aspect of organization that managers are often loath to discuss and about which information is not generally public.

There is some evidence nonetheless that a pattern might exist. In 2007 Shell Canada became 100 per cent owned by Royal Dutch Shell, which disbanded Shell Canada's independent board of directors in favour of its European board. Before that change, Shell Canada – like many Canadian companies – had avoided taking a strong stance, accepting only intensity targets at a limited level. Royal Dutch Shell, on the other hand, was actively examining future scenarios related to climate change and the likely future conditions for the firm if, as a Shell Canada official explained, a) "climate change events precede climate change action" (called the "scramble scenario") or b) "climate change action precedes climate change events" (called the "blueprint scenario"). Royal Dutch Shell ultimately came to believe that a scramble scenario would lead to such severe restrictions on its operations as to threaten the company's future. Its executives thus decided, according to the official I interviewed, that "the well-being of our company is best served by a blueprint scenario." The European company's preference for "climate change action" was a cap-and-trade program, an instrument with which it had substantial experience through the European Union Emissions

Trading System. Shell Canada's preference shifted to cap-and-trade at that time. Thus, in the case of Shell Canada, the individuals involved did appear to influence preferences.

Two points, however, call into question the significance of convictions and beliefs. First, the switch to the European board of directors also changed the experience on which the board was drawing. The Canadian board had no experience with any regulatory instrument, while the Royal Dutch Shell board by that time had had two years experience with emissions trading under the European system. It is possible, therefore, that the shift in preference had less to do with personal convictions and beliefs and more with a change in experience. Second, Royal Dutch Shell bought Shell Canada just as the shift in Canadian industry's preference towards carbon pricing occurred. It is likely, therefore, that some such change would have taken place at Shell Canada at that time even if its had remained independent.

The methodological challenges inherent in testing the convictions and beliefs variable thus include the inability to collect adequate data, and the difficulty of differentiating between the experience variable and the convictions and beliefs variable. The latter point highlights the fact that it is challenging even to define "convictions and beliefs." Certainly, it includes the ideas managers have about the policy instruments, but it is not immediately apparent where those ideas came from – an important point in helping us get at the actual source of preference change. Are convictions and beliefs of key managers merely a result of previous experience with the instrument, in which case the experience variable covers this more specifically? Or are they a result of personal and other professional experiences of managers, including their upbringing, culture, and education? Moreover, what types of convictions and beliefs matter? For the purpose of this analysis, I refer to "convictions and beliefs" as including the broad rage of ideas that managers have about the policy instruments, rather than those resulting from a firm's previous experience with a particular instrument. This is undoubtedly a broad category, which is another major limitation of the concept in this study.

Faced with these problems, the first step in examining the significance of personal convictions and beliefs was to determine if, after taking the competitive advantage and experience variables into account, there was anything left to explain. If the answer was yes, then further data collection was warranted. If the answer was no, then the issue was moot.

As it turns out, with respect to firms' preferences, of carbon-pricing instruments, almost all of the variation can be explained through either the advantage or the experience variable. Table 3 lists firms whose preferences can be explained by experience with, or the expectation of competitive advantage from, a particular instrument and those whose preferences remain unexplained.

The preferences of only five firms are not, at first glance, explained by either the advantage or experience variables – when the latter is defined as a positive correlation between experience and preference. Upon closer examination, however, experience did play a role in the

Table 3. Experience/Competitive Advantage with, and Preference of, Carbon-pricing Instruments, Selected Firms, Canada, 2009

Variation in Preference Explained by Experience or Competitive Advantage	
Firms with a competitive advantage from a carbon-pricing instrument that correlates with their preference	*Preference*
St. Mary's Cement	Cap-and-trade
Encana	Carbon tax
Union Gas	Carbon tax
AbitibiBowater	Cap-and-trade
Weyerhaeuser	Cap-and-trade
Firms with experience with one carbon-pricing instrument, but a competitive advantage from another	
West Fraser Timber	No preference
Canfor	No preference
Catalyst Paper	No preference
Firms with local experience with a carbon-pricing instrument that correlates with their preference	*Preference*
Suncor Energy	Cap-and-trade
AbitibiBowater	Cap-and-trade
Weyerhaeuser	Cap-and-trade
Shell Canada	Cap-and-trade
Holcim Canada	Cap-and-trade
Lehigh Cement	Cap-and-trade
TransAlta	Cap-and-trade
Variation in Preference Not Explained by Experience or Competitive Advantage	
Firms with local experience with a carbon-pricing instrument, but supporting the opposite instrument	*Preference*
Essroc (experience: cap-and-trade)	Carbon tax or voluntary
Firms with peripheral experience, supporting the opposite policy instrument	*Preference*
ConocoPhillips Canada	Carbon tax
Nexen	Carbon tax
Firms with no experience with or competitive advantage from a carbon-pricing instrument	*Preference*
Gaz Métro	Cap-and-trade
Petro-Canada	No preference

preference of one firm. Essroc's negative experience with cap-and-trade led the company's representative to believe that any future cap-and-trade program would have similar problems; in other words, the negative experience did provide certainty to the firm, but by causing it to abandon one possible policy instrument choice in favour of the alternatives. Consequently, although the familiarity effect appears generally to breed support for an instrument, the Essroc case reminds us that, if a policy instrument is implemented badly in one instance, a firm might not support it in others.

Thus, of the eighteen firms in this study,[16] the preferences of only four cannot be explained by competitive advantage or previous experience. It is possible, therefore, that, in the absence of advantage or local experience, managers draw on their personal convictions or beliefs about a policy instrument and its effects. More research, however, would be required to determine the extent of that effect, since the study's data set is small. A larger data set would allow for multiple regression analysis, which could determine whether one could attribute the remaining effect to convictions and beliefs when other variables are held constant. That said, a more nuanced definition would also likely be required, one that more clearly defines the types of convictions and beliefs under discussion. Without a larger data set, however, this is not possible and so, for the purposes of this study, the significance of this variable is considered null.

In addition, the increased support for carbon tax in the sample of "unexplained" firms suggests that a continuing research agenda should examine whether firms with no advantage from or local experience with a particular carbon-pricing instrument are more likely to prefer carbon taxation. If a larger sample demonstrated that this was the case, the finding might further support the significance of the familiarity effect, since taxation in general is a policy instrument with which firms have considerable experience, even if carbon taxation per se would be new.

In sum, it appears that the convictions and beliefs of key managers had little if any effect on the preferences of climate change policy instruments of firms in this study. This does not mean, however, that the ideas of managers are of no import. During the course of the study, a correlation was implied between managers' perceptions of risk – as

---

16 As in Chapter 6, I include TransAlta here, but not in the summary in Chapter 1, as it was not strictly a participating firm.

relating to short-term profits versus long-term expected profits – and the level of environmental engagement undertaken by the firm. In other words, firms whose managers thought of climate change policy instrument risks as affecting only the next quarter or next year's profits were far less proactive than those that took a longer-term view. For the latter group, climate change policy in general and their specific policy instrument choices were much more a matter of survival for the firm. In both cases, the concern was that profits would fall, but the latter group perceived a greater threat to the firm and was therefore more proactive.

These findings are of interest because they speak to the wider literature on corporate social responsibility and why firms would adopt environmental practices in the absence of cost savings. Much of the literature originally examined how firms can gain competitive advantage from environmental actions, but recent work has argued that not all environmental practices provide an advantage (for a summary, see Gunningham 2009). So why do firms adopt such policies? Gunningham, Kagan, and Thornton (2004) argue that firms might take action to protect their "license to operate," which for these authors goes well beyond the regulations set by government and includes social, economic, and regulatory demands on the firm from stakeholders, including community members and shareholders. As Gunningham explains, this makes corporate decision-making on the environment complex and, as found here in relation to policy preferences, firms might act more progressively to reduce risk:

> [T]his research also found that terms of each strand of the "license to operate" are often far from clear. Different corporate managers may interpret similar regulatory, economic or social demands differently, and with them their position as regards CER [corporate enviornmental responsibility]. For example, how far is it rational for an enterprise to go in reducing environmental risk, particularly when risk-reducing measures are costly and seemingly unprofitable? This, they found, depends very much on how an enterprise *perceives* those risks and on "environmental management style." (Gunningham 2009, 226; emphasis in original)

More research is again required, however, to unpack how different managers interpret environmental risks differently and, therefore, why different firms in the same industry might adopt wildly different strategies in relation to the environment. The following analysis suggests that there is a temporal component to how managers perceive risk and, therefore, to their firm's interest in adopting corporate social responsibility.

Long-Run versus Short-Run Perspectives of Risk

The distinction between the long run and the short run is significant in microeconomics. The short run is a period when many fixed commitments (such as contracts or leases) dictate a firm's decision-making; in the long run, all commitments are variable. In the short run, fixed costs might make entry into or exit from a market challenging. In the long run, however, a firm can enter the market in response to long-term expected profits and it can leave that market in response to losses.

The distinction between the long-run and short-run is useful here because it highlights two potentially different interpretations of risk related to climate change policy instruments. Managers with a short-run perspective might view the firm's current commitments, the firm's current profits, and the current configuration of the market, as preventing any major upset. Climate change policy instruments, therefore, would represent another increased cost but would not be viewed as representing much of a threat. In the long run, however, everything can change, and a firm could lose its market share or even be forced out of the market due to changes brought on by, say, climate change policy instruments. A firm with a short-run view, therefore, might respond to investors' concerns by adopting a preference for an expected policy instrument, but it would limit its action as much as possible. A firm with a long-run view, however, would see the risks associated with climate change policy instruments as threatening its survival, warranting strong action.

This difference in managerial perspective might help to explain the differences in major firms' environmental actions, and why some firms are leaders while others are laggards. Certainly, the evidence from this study suggests a correlation between a long-run perspective and greater environmental action. The finding has a significant limitation, however, in that there were not enough laggard firms in the data set to provide a reliable test of the hypothesis. Moreover, although I assume here that long-run and short-run perspectives are ideational, other material explanations – for instance, that a firm has more long-run capital-intensive stock than do its competitors – might also explain managers' perspectives. Nonetheless, here I lay out the evidence for each industry in the study, and at the end of the chapter I discuss the limitations of the findings.

Cement

In the cement industry, a long-term perspective appears to have been prevalent from an early stage. In 1999 ten of the world's biggest cement companies formed the Cement Sustainability Initiative (CSI) under the rubric of the World Business Council for Sustainable Issues. The group has since expanded to twenty-five members. All of the cement firms that participated in this study were members of the organization.

The initial group commissioned a $4 million research project on the "long-term sustainability" of the industry from Battelle Memorial Institute in the United States (Klee and Coles 2004). Independent observers, including Mostafa Tolba, former executive director of the United Nations Environment Programme, monitored the venture. The report, entitled *Toward a Sustainable Cement Industry*, published in March 2002, called for a number of changes in the industry (Battelle Memorial Institute 2002). In response, CSI members published an action plan entitled *Our Agenda for Action* in July 2003 "to fundamentally examine and change the way in which [the cement industry] does business" (Klee and Coles 2004).

The founding of the CSI was directly related to the recognition by leading cement firms that, in a low-carbon future, the viability of cement as a product and the industry as a business would be questionable. According to Howard Klee, CSI project manager, and co-author Elaine Coles: "This was of course not simply an altruistic decision – it is an acknowledgement by the participating companies that their 'license to operate,' competitiveness, profitability and ultimately long-term survival are inextricably linked to meeting their environmental and corporate social responsibilities" Klee and Coles 2004, 115). Had there been any doubt of this fact when the initial group formed in 1999? "[T]he [Battelle] report's message to the cement industry was unambiguous – the industry needs to change in order to ensure its long-term survival and success" (Klee and Coles 2004, 116).

As most cement firms are headquartered in Europe, where climate change became a salient issue much sooner (Lorenzoni and Pidgeon 2006), the industry acted far earlier than did North American manufacturers, according to Robert Page, chair of the National Round Table on the Environment and the Economy. Canadian subsidiaries subsequently adopted their parent company's preference, which explains the comfort with which cement firms' representatives spoke of cap-and trade. Only one firm, Essroc (a subsidiary of Italcementi), supported a carbon tax due to concerns over possible speculation in a carbon market, according to VP Environmental Affairs Gary Molchan.

The cement industry, perceiving the risks of climate change over the long run, moved early to adapt to climate change regulation. This perception of risk related to climate change likely was linked to the same forces I discussed in Chapters 3 and 4 – namely, public opinion and investors' expectations of regulatory policy changes. These European-based cement firms' perceptions of threat, therefore, would be related to the policy climate and public opinion in Europe. Unlike in North America, by the mid-1990s between 84 and 89 per cent of Europeans were reported as being very or quite worried about climate change (Lorenzoni and Pidgeon 2006). Moreover, by the late 1990s the signing of the Kyoto Protocol and European governments' proactive stances would have been expected to increase public and investors' expectations of greater regulatory action. Thus, faced with a new policy climate that could threaten their long-term viability, cement firms as a group reacted proactively, not obstructively, to adapt to the new business environment.

Petroleum

In the petroleum industry there was much more variation among firms' responses to climate change, with both leaders and laggards. The reason for the variation might be differences in managers' perceptions of the risks associated with climate change as affecting either short-term profits or long-term expected profits.

Certainly, evidence from this study points to this pattern, although unavoidable limitations of the data set prevent a conclusive result. Four firms – ConocoPhillips Canada, Suncor Energy, Nexen, and Shell Canada – were extremely proactive with respect to climate change: defining clear preferences, articulating those preferences publicly, hiring staff to deal with climate change directly, and creating public communications on the issue, among other things. Managers at these firms did perceive the regulatory threats associated with climate change in very broad terms, using language that demonstrated a concern for their firm's long-term survival. Those from Shell Canada, ConocoPhillips Canada, and Suncor Energy pointed to possible market closures and product bans due to the environmental impact of the oil sands. Nexen's representative Wishart Robson talked about the possibility of higher costs leading to hostile acquisitions due to the falling share prices associated with climate policy:

When I talk about shareholders, it's just a recognition that it's not our money, it's their money. So, they expect and deserve a competitive rate of return. If they don't get it, you run the risk of having them withdraw their funds and having them go invest in someone else. Where you get into real big differences for what the cost of producing a barrel of oil is here versus the cost of producing a barrel of oil in the United States, you get into competition issues. And, if you are interested in investing in the oil and gas sector and you are going to get a more competitive rate of return from investing in Hess or in El Paso or some equivalent American organization or somewhere else, investors may choose to do that, and then you end up with Canadian companies being disadvantaged. Their credit rating goes down, their share price goes down, they still have reserves, someone comes along and takes them out.

Thus, for each of these firms, climate change merited attention largely because it could undermine the viability of the firm over the long-run.

The fifth petroleum firm in this study, Petro-Canada, purposely avoided a proactive stance on the issue. Its representative explained:

If we don't see a benefit [to declaring a preference] but we see risk, then we are not going to publicly disclose things. In those kinds of things, in reputation management ... like a Nexen or a Suncor who may not have a direct link – well, in Nexen's case, no real link – to the gas pumps, they can say whatever they want and the public [can't respond]. Particularly Nexen can say, "oh yeah, we love carbon tax" because they don't have customers that are going to *not* go to their gas station. So, Petro-Canada's behaviour was really based on [the fact that] we're Canada's gas station: we have fifteen hundred gas stations across Canada. Given that we started as a Crown corporation, if an email went around [stating], "lets boycott gas stations," well, what gas station would they boycott? Petro-Canada. So, we would manage our reputation very carefully. So, there is really no benefit to Petro-Canada coming out publicly and saying we're in favour of a carbon tax or we're in favour of a cap-and-trade.

The claim that Petro-Canada avoided taking a stance on climate change is supported by the corporation's annual reports, which do not mention the issue until 2008, much later and far less often than the reports of the other participating petroleum firms. Petro-Canada, according to the official I interviewed, was happy to allow the Canadian Association of Petroleum Producers to deal with the issue in its stead, and supported any action the association viewed as necessary.

Petro-Canada's policy of avoidance corresponded with a lack of concern on the part of the firm's representative about the implications of climate change policy instruments for its long-run viability. The interviewee stated that the firm's climate change strategy "was really risk mitigation," and defined risk in terms of increased or variable costs. When asked if this could threaten the firm's long-run survival, however, the official responded, "no, because supply and demand would kick in." From Petro-Canada's perspective, the interviewee argued, the firm would merely pass on the cost to consumers and, unless there was a change in demand, the long-term viability of the corporation would not be threatened. Thus, without a long-run perspective, the firm saw "no benefit" in proactively taking a stance on climate change. Instead, it saw a proactive strategy as risky, but solely in terms of lower short-term profits if consumers disliked its stance.

Interview subjects at the proactive firms also supported the hypothesis that their less-proactive counterparts conceived of risk in a short-term, rather than a long-term, perspective. A Shell Canada representative described that company's perspective on climate change policy as "[in a] scenario where we don't act for five to ten years, when action happens it will be so severe and draconian that it will be very damaging to the company, our interests, to our shareholders ... We intend to develop the oil sands resource. Ten years from now, if climate change has not been addressed, people might say, 'well, no, I'm afraid you can't develop that oil sands resource anymore.' So, we think it's best for us to take action and take action now in a meaningful way."

A ban on oil sands development would leave Shell Canada and other petroleum firms in Canada with a sizeable stranded asset that could seriously affect their long-term expect profits and even their survival. Whether a firm perceived this threat as probable, therefore, would affect whether it adopted a proactive strategy with respect to climate change. The Shell Canada representative believed that inactive firms "must come up with different visions in terms of planning and how long they are planning for," and suggested that a company such as Exxon – "probably today the most successful oil and gas company in operation from a revenue and profitability perspective" – must feel that, given its current success, the best strategy would be to advocate the status quo and avoid increased costs as long as possible. The difference between these companies, said the Shell Canada official, is "risk and it's also being broader minded in your thinking in terms of what influences will make you a successful company or an unsuccessful company."

Consequently, interview data from the petroleum sector also suggest that proactive companies viewed the risks of climate change from a long-run perspective. Indeed, the only petroleum firm in the study that adopted a policy of avoidance took the opposite perspective. Moreover, the data suggest that this phenomenon was not unique to the firms that participated in this study.

TransAlta

For this study I interviewed Robert Page, former senior executive at the electricity-generating company, TransAlta, in his capacity as chair of the National Round Table on the Environment and the Economy. I use his remarks to augment the data from other industries.

TransAlta is often cited as a leader on climate change among firms in Canada. Supporting the data from other industries, Page suggested that the firm's proactive strategy was due largely to concern for its own long-term survival:

> For some companies, they look at the bottom line as something on a year-by-year basis, and what's really critical is what will the numbers be for the next quarter, the next half, the next year. That's what drives the share price and, therefore, that's the only thing [they] should really be [looking at]. Something out five years, ten years, fifteen years, then, is not something that [they are] going to be concerned about. The proactive school says, "look, unless I'm working on public policy, or public attitudes, or new technology development or innovation and this kind of thing, because its all interrelated, then I'm going to get hit and I'm going to get hit hard." TransAlta has been in business for a hundred years and they view themselves as wanting to be in business for another hundred years.

As a coal-fired electricity generator, TransAlta – like cement producers and proactive oil producers – saw climate change as something that, in the long run, could undermine its business model. Increased public concern about climate change might lead governments to limit or ultimately to ban the use of coal, and reputational concerns could affect the firm's revenue. Page argued that many firms have learned this lesson from recent environmental scandals:

> Risk is more than just a financial question. Risk brings in the issue of the brand. You know, the *Exxon Valdez*, had it [belonged to] a smaller

company, could have easily put Exxon into bankruptcy because at one point the liability was over six billion dollars ... They had the resources to cover that, [but] many companies wouldn't have. [In addition,] when you had the *Exxon Valdez*, a whole group of people publicly sent in their credit cards chopped up ... When your corporate brand for environmental, or safety or health reasons gets a real whack, then that in turn hits you in terms of your market sales. People back away from buying your product in connection with it.

To forestall possible product bans and brand implications, not only in Canada but also in the United States, TransAlta became active: decreasing emissions, buying emissions credits, and taking part in emissions credit trades from an early period. Page contended that, having had a positive experience with these endeavours, the firm remained committed to emissions trading as its preferred climate change policy instrument.

Limitations of the Data

Although the observations support the hypothesis that managers' different perspectives of risk – that is, whether they take a long-run or short-run view – affect the environmental actions of large firms, the available data clearly have limitations.

First, there is only one non-proactive company, Petro-Canada, in the sample. It is consequently difficult to generalize to other non-proactive firms based on evidence from a single case.

Second, the former Petro-Canada official whom I interviewed agreed to speak to me only after the firm had been taken over by Suncor Energy, and it is difficult to be certain that the official could speak for the firm. Consequently, although the above statements do indicate Petro-Canada's policy before 2009 with regard to climate change, they are less reliable than those of petroleum executives who had the authority and authorization to speak for an operational firm. Unfortunately, all of those officials were from firms with a proactive policy. The reason for the lack of more inactive companies, however, was not that I intentionally sought out only proactive firms, but that so-called laggard companies – such as Imperial Oil, Total, Husky, Canadian Natural Resources Limited, and Synenco – either refused to participate or did not respond to my request. It would be inappropriate to label the level of activity of these firms without either interview data or further primary research, but none of these firms, unlike the proactive firms that participated, was viewed as an environmental leader by interview subjects from government, non-governmental organizations, or other firms.

It could be, however, that a firm's refusal to discuss its climate change preference and actions publicly went hand in hand with an inactive strategy. Indeed, an official at Imperial Oil – a subsidiary of Exxon Mobil well known for its obstructionist behaviour with respect to climate change – explained that he could not submit to an interview because it was the company's policy not to discuss internal decisions. The former Petro-Canada representative confirmed that this had also been that firm's policy: "Our 'preference' was not to be in favour of any kind of policy. And that's frankly ... the way Petro-Canada operated. We were very tight about what we would communicate publicly, which is probably why you were having difficulty getting someone to talk to you."

The third limitation of the data is that it was beyond the scope of this study to determine why managers at some firms adopted a long-run perspective while those at other firms adopt a short-run view. I interpreted this finding as indicating the views of the firm's chief executive on environmental actions or as expressing the firm's corporate culture. It is equally possible, however, that the reason is differences in firms' characteristics: managers in firms with more long-run capital stock might take a longer-run view, for instance. Again, further study is needed to determine how firms' decisions on addressing the climate change issue are made.

Chapter Nine

Conclusions

I began this book with an empirical puzzle: why did leading Canadian firms and business associations declare support for a carbon price over less costly voluntary climate change policy instruments? I conclude with an empirically validated model from which I argue that business preferences for such policy instruments are determined by managers through an analysis of three central factors: the risks the policy instrument implies for the firm's capital investments, the likely effect of the instrument on the risk perceptions of external investors, and, finally, any possible advantage the instrument might offer the firm. As these analyses ultimately require managers to make predictions about an uncertain future, they are affected strongly by expectations of future government policy choices. Is regulatory change likely? If so, what instruments might be implemented? What effects would those instruments have on the firm? Expectations about the likelihood and form of regulatory change are influenced by the political context, while the firm's previous experience with a policy instrument strongly influences managers' perceptions of the effects that the instrument would have on the firm.

I responded to the empirical puzzle by asking the research question: what causes variation in business preferences for climate change policy instruments over time and among firms and industry associations? The model's answer is that variations *over time* are caused by changes in the political context – changes that create uncertainty about the regulatory environment and, thus, investment risk. Variations in preferences *among firms and associations* are the result of two factors: differences in the potential competitive advantage that a policy instrument might create for a firm or industry, and differences in firms' previous experience with particular policy instruments.

The effects of both the political context and past experience mean that business preferences are shaped by the actions of past governments and the prospects of actions by future governments. Business preferences in this domain are thus mutable and endogenous to the business-government relationship itself, rather than fixed and exogenous. This finding not only contributes to our understanding of the Canadian case; it also lays the foundation for further research into business-government relations more broadly.

Summary of the Canadian Case and Contributions

This research program was originally conceived as a study of business influence on climate change policy in Canada. The unconscious assumption at the root of the enterprise was that business was somehow to blame, likely due to the need to avoid cost, for Canada's continuing failure to take substantial action to reduce its growing greenhouse gas emissions. By understanding how business influenced government in Canada, an understudied area of research, policy-makers and environmentalists might be able to overcome this influence and get Canada finally to take meaningful action on climate change.

Then, in January 2008, news from Ottawa highlighted not only that this assumption was unproven, but also that it might be inherently flawed. The National Round Table on the Environment and the Economy (NRTEE) had called for a carbon price – erroneously reported in the media as specific support for a carbon tax. The federal government was derisive, while the opposition responded by reiterating its support for cap-and-trade. The NRTEE's only outright defenders that day came from the business community and, indeed, from two of the country's most powerful business groups: the Canadian Council of Chief Executives and the Canadian Association of Petroleum Producers.

This turn of events threw into question the very viability, in addition to the utility, of a study of business influence on climate change policy at that time. Were business preferences actually affecting the Canadian government's climate change policies? How could we know if business was exerting influence on policy outcomes without first knowing what business actually wanted when it came to climate change policy? The one was a prerequisite to the other.

The research I have presented in this book, therefore, furthers the study of business-government relations on environmental policy in Canada. By focusing on the policy instrument preferences of business – what business wants from government and why – I hope I have increased the clarity of the incentives and motives of the side of the business-government relationship that generally has received less attention in the study of Canadian public policy, and in so doing established a foundation for future study of business influence in this area.

My research demonstrates that, in deciding to support one policy instrument over another, firms seek not only to limit compliance costs, but also to ensure cost predictability and stability and, where possible, to gain advantage. Where an expectation of regulatory change creates regulatory instability – in the sense that a firm does not know what its regulatory costs will be during the lifespan of its investments – a firm will adopt a preference for the policy instruments it deems most likely to be implemented, thereby creating a new stable regulatory environment. In Canada, large businesses supported the least expensive and most predictable policy instruments – voluntary agreements and subsidies – for fifteen years, until public opinion created strong expectations of regulatory change among both firms' managers and investors. The status quo then became viewed as transitory and not to be relied upon as relevant to future investment decisions, either within firms or by external investors. Creating a new regulatory equilibrium, therefore, required that government implement a new policy as soon as possible, and large business in Canada, almost *en masse*, changed their preference to the policy instrument deemed most likely – namely, carbon pricing – even though carbon-pricing instruments would be far more expensive than voluntary agreements and subsidies.

In choosing between probable policy instruments – in this case, types of carbon-pricing instruments – firms obviously preferred instruments that offer an advantage over competitors. Where no such advantage existed, however, firms faced a conundrum: should they believe the proponents of grandfathered cap-and-trade, who argue that option is the most flexible and least costly, or the proponents of carbon taxation, who suggest that instrument is the simplest, most efficient, and most predictable? In other words, should firms support the least expensive policy instrument or the one that offers the most predictable costs? Given the difficulty in deciding between these two negative choices, firms generally adopted a preference for the instrument they had already experienced in other jurisdictions. I argue that this is because managers saw the effects of the previously experienced instrument as more certain than those of the alternatives. They were able to judge for themselves the policy instrument's likely effect on the firm and, consequently, were more likely to support that instrument. This tendency even decreased the effect of competitive advantage where a firm had experience with one instrument but a theoretical advantage from another.

Next Steps: Future Research Opportunities

Testing Generalizability

Where do we go from here? The risk-advantage model – developed from the answers that senior managers, policy-makers, and representatives of non-governmental organizations gave to questions about business policy preferences – clarifies the decision-making framework managers use in determining policy preferences. A subsequent test of that model demonstrated that, with one exception, it was indeed useful in explaining business preferences for climate change policy instruments in Canada over time and across sectors. It could therefore be useful in understanding business preferences for public policy instruments in other policy areas and jurisdictions.

Demonstrating the generalizability of the model, however, will require further research. The varieties of capitalism literature warns us that findings related to the Canadian political economy might be relevant only in Canada and other liberal market economies, such as the United Kingdom, the United States, Australia, and New Zealand. The particular structure of the Canadian economy makes corporate governance and relationships with investors a much more significant factor than in the coordinated market economies common in Europe. Nonetheless, *prima face* evidence suggests that, at least in other liberal market economies, such an exercise might prove fruitful.

Indeed, the key variables highlighted by the model – particularly the significance of certainty, policy expectations, and investors' concerns – could help explain some of the more puzzling events in US climate politics since 2008. From 2008 to 2010, a number of US lawmakers worked to develop a cap-and-trade system, but ultimately failed to achieve their goal. During this period, three US petroleum firms – Shell, ConocoPhillips, and BP – proposed that transportation emissions be covered in the system through an unorthodox policy instrument called a "linked fee" under which firms would buy allowances for the carbon content in their product (Lizza 2010). Exxon Mobil had previously proposed such a fee in a letter to the Western Climate Initiative (WCI) in 2008 (Stuewer 2008). The fee would be paid on the average price of gasoline each firm sold, and be based on the average cost of carbon in the cap-and-trade system over the previous three months (Lizza 2010). Ultimately, in the spring of 2010, the American Petroleum Institute, the association representing US oil and natural gas producers, agreed to support the idea, demonstrating a level of unanimity in the US industry that has not been apparent in its Canadian counterpart.

Interestingly, Shell and ConocoPhillips previously had supported a traditional cap-and-trade program in the United States or internationally, while Exxon Mobil was known for its obstructionist actions – including hiring those who dismiss concerns about climate change – although it has more recently declared a preference for taxation (Clark 2009). Why were these firms' preferences coalescing around the unorthodox idea of a linked carbon fee? When one takes into account expectations for US climate policy, in addition to industry's need to limit risk and create certainty, the linked fee might be seen to offer a good risk-mitigation strategy for firms.

Unlike in Canada, in the United States almost all cap-and-trade proposals included a component to cover transportation fuels by forcing suppliers or refiners to hold credits for the carbon in that fuel. Consequently, US oil companies expected that any cap-and-trade program would ensure a new and unknown cost of production, most likely at the refining or distribution stage (Pew Center on Global Climate Change 2008). Moreover, cap-and-trade would give firms little ability to manage the risks associated with the new cost, given that it would be determined in a new market without a clear history or pattern of volatility from which to predict future costs. In a perspective that mirrored that of the Canadian Petroleum Products Institute, US firms were concerned that this inability to plan for or control costs would undermine the US refining industry in favour of its global competitors (Lizza 2010).

Thus, the linked fee had two benefits. First, compared to a volatile, market-based cap-and-trade program, it would have given firms some certainty over pricing, at least over a three-month term. Second, instead of paying major sums to other industries to buy credits through cap-and-trade, the petroleum industry conceivably could have gained access to some of those funds, paid to government, through other programs or tax cuts. Exxon Mobil described this possibility in its letter to the WCI in 2008:

> Given WCI's choice to implement a cap-and-trade on large stationary emitters of [greenhouse gases], Exxon Mobil supports addressing fossil

transportation fuels through a market-determined carbon fee, rather than direct inclusion in the cap-and-trade program. The carbon fee should be equivalent to the cost of carbon in the cap-and-trade program, with *recycle of the revenue through a broad-based reduction of a current tax on labor or capital*. The linkage could be accomplished efficiently by basing the fee on the average cost of carbon in the industrial cap-and-trade program during a recent period of time. This "linked fee" approach *will ensure a consistent price of carbon in the market (unlike [low carbon fuel standard] or biofuels mandates) while minimizing market instability, price volatility and the potential for supply disruptions.* (Stuewer 2008; emphasis added)

The most significant variable in the equation, however, was certainty, particularly price stability, which explains a turn of events that puzzled even lawmakers. After it became clear that the linked fee would come under attack by media and political opponents as a new gas tax, lawmakers proposed a new option: firms would buy permits, which government would sell at a stable price outside the normal cap-and-trade system. To the surprise of policy-makers, industry showed no reticence in agreeing (Lizza 2010). Ultimately the new option was both more probable *and* might even have provided greater certainty about costs over a longer period. Although the coalition behind the US cap-and-trade system ultimately fell apart in late April 2010, the US petroleum industry's preference for a linked fee over the previously expected cap-and-trade program demonstrates the *prima face* utility of the model in understanding firms' climate change policy instrument preferences in other jurisdictions.

Questions remain, however, particularly about the generalizability of the model to other policy areas. Although the varieties of capitalism framework suggests the significance of relationships with investors in liberal market economies, Hall and Soskice (2003) list four other "spheres" that might cause firms coordination problems. Relationships with other stakeholders – employees, unions, other firms, educational institutions – predominant in these spheres could also have a considerable effect on business policy preferences. Does the structure of Canada's political economy mean that investors will *always* represent the most significant relational problem Canadian firms face, or is it the specific characteristics of climate change policy instruments that lead to the pre-eminence of investors in the minds of decision-makers grappling with that topic? Would business leaders grappling with other policy areas – employment equity, trade, health and safety – use similar decision-making analyses? Answering this question requires determining if the model developed here is generalizable to other policy issue areas.

Confirming the Findings: Expanding n

Given the limited availability of previous research into business preferences for public policy in Canada, qualitative methods seemed the best way to solve the empirical puzzle. After all, the most appropriate way to figure out what Canadian firms wanted and why was to ask them, through their senior officials, directly. Interviewing other members of the Canadian climate change policy community outside industry provided corroborating evidence on business perspectives and actions. This type of research – focused directly on the development of policy instrument preferences – had not been undertaken previously in Canada.

Qualitative research, however, comes with its own trade-offs and limitations. Undoubtedly, creating this model required a level of interpretation in finding patterns in the data provided by sixty interview respondents. To overcome this challenge, the subsequent model-testing phase – the conclusion of which is laid out in Chapters 3 to 7 – was needed to ensure the model's validity in explaining the case. The model passed these tests with one exception: the significance of convictions and beliefs could not be confirmed.

Still, it cannot be denied that this study's sample size is relatively small. In the forestry and cement industries, this is partially because the Canadian industry itself is small – for instance, the Cement Association of Canada has only nine member firms – while in the petroleum sector it was extremely difficult to get companies to respond despite significant attempts to expand the sample. Moreover, interview collection is a time-consuming and resource-intensive process, which in itself limits the number of data points. Nonetheless, a larger sample size would have increased the reliability of the findings.

Although I deemed a small-n case study format the best methodology to unravel the puzzle at this juncture, the next step in this research agenda might be to test the findings through a quantitative analysis with a larger data set. This would provide an opportunity to examine further certain specific implications of the model, including the link between experience, competitive advantage, and specific policy preferences, as well as the possible significance of convictions and beliefs about climate change for firms without experience with a carbon-pricing instrument or expectations of a competitive advantage from one. More-over, a quantitative study could provide further support for the gener-alizability of the model across firms in different sectors, which in this study were represented only by their associations.

Nonetheless, the small-*n*, qualitative methodology I used here proved fruitful in providing an opportunity for theory-building in a generally undeveloped area of research in Canadian public policy. Had this research begun as a quantitative analysis, it is quite possible that the significance of risk as a concept and of investment in general would have been missed.

This case study research also demonstrates the utility of viewing the firm, not as unitary actor, but as a composite actor in which decisions are based on interactions among decision-makers (Prakash 2000). In doing so, it opens space for ideational components in decision-making, while not negating the significance of market factors and the incentives inherent in the structure of the economy. This does not mean that it is never useful to assume a firm is a unitary actor; rather, empirical case study research, which can highlight the complex interactions of leaders in decision-making, can also be fruitful.

New Avenues for Future Research

The patterns of firms' decision-making and behaviour I have examined in this book also highlight specific issues in business-government rela-tions on the environment that require further study. I described one such research area in Chapter 7: the possible link between managers' perceptions of climate change policy risk – from a long- or short-run perspective – and variations in firms' willingness to act on the environ-ment. Would the findings of that chapter – that firms appear more will-ing to act progressively on the environment when they take a long-run perspective – bear out in a wider and more diverse data set?

Another area of further research relates to the effects of policy learn-ing and norm diffusion on firms' preferences for policy instruments. The story of preferences for climate change policy instruments in Can-ada demonstrates that industry, while diverse in products and pro-cesses, can exhibit an extraordinary amount of homogeneity. With only limited exceptions, the Canadian business community adopted similar preferences for approximately fifteen years, and then shifted those pref-erences in the same approximate period in response to public opinion. The main reason for this homogeneity is that firms, in any sector, face similar incentives and obstacles vis-à-vis investment. This does not negate, however, a role for learning and norm diffusion in preparing business officials to view a public opinion shift as an indicator of significant shareholder concern and increased likelihood of policy change. Moreover, it might help explain why firms almost unanimously supported a carbon price, not traditional command-and-control regulation. Indeed, learning and dialogue could play a considerable role in creating consensus among industry officials in their interpretations of the policy issue and their expectations regarding the possibility of regulatory change. This link, however, remains elusive.

The existence of the Industry Steering Committee on Climate Change (ISC3), a group made up of representatives of Canadian business associations and large firms, particularly highlights this possibility. Several interview subjects cited the ISC3, created in the late 1990s, as providing a forum for debate, learning, and collaboration. In this regard, the semi-formal organization could represent a "deliberative institution," which Hall and Soskice argue industry will develop to "enhance the capacity of actors in the political economy for strategic action when faced with new or unfamiliar challenges" (2009, 30). Certainly, ISC3 provided a forum in which firms and associations could grapple with climate change as a group, cutting across sectors and organizations, at a time when industry understanding of the policy implications and science was in its infancy. Further research into ISC3's role, therefore, could help to explain the link between policy learning and the decision-making framework described here.

One additional research area requires further attention. In this book, I portrayed communication between the firm and its shareholders as similar to that between government and its constituents: firms take the temperature of shareholders through public opinion, then respond through mass-marketing documents such as annual reports. Institutional investors and creditors, on the other hand, can articulate their views directly to firms in meetings and other direct communications. Thus, although institutional investors have a clear voice, shareholders' perceptions can be inferred only through public opinion.

This conceptualization of shareholder-firm interaction undoubtedly has much truth, but organizations that offer intelligence and advice to shareholders could be vehicles for more direct communications. Proxy firms, such as Institutional Shareholder Services and Glass Lewis and Co., provide advice and rankings of firms to assist shareholders' decision-making. It would be incorrect to suggest that these firms speak for shareholders – since they do not attempt to provide any actual representation – but their reports might provide another way, in addition to public opinion, for firms to gauge shareholders' concerns. Consequently, further research and theorizing is required to understand the role of external investors in public policy. Shareholders' influence, as referenced in this book, is undoubtedly less complex than the reality. A more nuanced understanding of the investor as a political actor is likely required.

The Final Word

Through this study we've learned that there is a third person at the table when business and government negotiate on climate change policy in Canada: the investor. Explicating the logic of investment, and particularly the need for policy certainty to decrease the risk inherent in investment, clarifies the rationale behind business preferences for climate change policy instruments. Firms protect their reputations to ensure investors' confidence while simultaneously making investment decisions within a regulatory environment dictated by government. As society moves towards more stringent environmental policy instruments, firms prefer that change happen sooner, rather than later, to establish a new regulatory equilibrium and so facilitate investment.

Business preferences, therefore, are influenced by the political context in which they are developed. The findings I have presented here offer a basis for understanding and even predicting business behaviour vis-à-vis government under diverse political conditions. The key variables I have highlighted – policy certainty, expectations of future government policy, experience with and expected competitive advantage from particular instruments, and investors' concerns – provide a foundation for explaining or predicting how business will react when the political and policy environment changes.

We are now several years removed from the interviews, and a decade removed from the initial shift in business policy preferences in 2006–07. Undoubtedly, the near-term regulatory expectations of all actors grappling with these issues have changed at least twice over the past decade. By 2011 the failure of the US Congress to pass legislation developing a cap-and-trade program and the Harper government's continued unwillingness to act unilaterally altered the regulatory environment for Canadian firms and associations, creating uncertainty in the short term. At the same time, the failure to generate political support in the United

States for the Keystone XL pipeline project, largely because of concerns about carbon emissions from the oil sands, frustrated the petroleum industry. Coupled with increased incidences of extreme weather events, which kept climate change on the minds of policy-makers, the public, and investors, it is unlikely that the expectation for an eventual carbon price ever completely disappeared. With the defeat of Mr Harper in 2015 by a party that campaigned on carbon pricing, the regulatory environment shifted again. The Trudeau government's September 2016 move to impose a minimum, national carbon price on provinces that do not adopt their own pricing mechanism bore out expectations, born in 2006, that all firms would eventually face carbon regulation, likely carbon pricing, no matter where in Canada they operate. At the time of writing, it is not yet clear how major firms and industry associations will react.

The pattern I have explored in this book suggests that Canadian firms will adapt their support to the most certain policy instruments. While firms and associations may decry the Trudeau government's initial patchwork policy, as inter-provincial corporations would face higher administrative costs in dealing with multiple systems and increased regulatory uncertainty due to the multiple governments involved,[17] they are likely to once again articulate support for a clear and certain carbon pricing initiative. Indeed, this research suggests there is likely to be some relief among business leaders that government is finally getting on with the inevitable.

Ultimately, big business should not be assumed to be the enemy of strong environmental policy. Given expectations of regulatory change, and clear indications of concern on the part of investors, the firms and industry associations in this study demanded more stringent environmental regulations in 2009 than government was willing to provide. Considering the significance of policy certainty and investment to business success, this stance was not altruism, nor was it irrational: it was good business sense.

---

17 Although on 3 November 2015, John Manley, President and CEO of the Business Council of Canada (formerly CCCE), wrote in a commentary on IPolitics entitled *Trudeau Wants to Get Serious about Climate Change: This Is How He Should Start*, "Recognizing that several provinces already have moved ahead with carbon-pricing initiatives, the role of the federal government should be to ensure reasonably consistent treatment across the country." The government appears to have adopted this approach.

Appendix: List of Interviews

Firm or Industry Association	Interview Subject
1 AbitibiBowater	Martin Fairbank, Manager, Energy Development and Strategy
2 Aluminum Association of Canada	Confidential
3 Canadian Association of Petroleum Producers	Pierre Alvarez, former president
4 Canadian Association of Petroleum Producers	Richard Hyndman, Senior Advisor on Climate Change
5 Canadian Chemical Producers' Association	Gordon Lloyd, Vice President, Technical Affairs
6 Canadian Chemical Producers' Association	Richard Paton, President and CEO
7 Canadian Council of Chief Executives	John Dillon, Vice President, Regulatory Affairs and General Counsel
8 Canadian Electricity Association	Pierre Guimond, President
9 Canadian Electricity Association	Victoria Christie, Senior Advisor Environmental Affairs
10 Canadian Gas Association	Mike Cleland, President and CEO
11 Canadian Petroleum Products Institute	Tony Macerollo, Public and Government Affairs
12 Canadian Steel Producers Association	Confidential
13 Canadian Vehicle Manufacturers' Association	Mark Nantais, President
14 Canfor	Mike Bradley, Director Technology
15 Catalyst Paper	Lyn Brown, Vice President Corporate Relations and Social Responsibility
16 Cement Association of Canada	Bob Masterson, Director of Policy
17 ConocoPhillips Canada	Bob Mitchell, Manager Climate Change
18 ConocoPhillips Canada	Dale Austin, Director Climate Change Business Frameworks
19 Delphi Group	Joe Rogers, Technical Manager
20 Delphi Group	Mike Gerbis, CEO

Continued

Firm or Industry Association	Interview Subject
21 Encana	Gerry Protti
22 Environment Canada	Confidential
23 Environment Canada	Confidential
24 Environment Canada	Confidential
25 Environment Canada	Confidential
26 Environment Canada	Confidential
27 Environment Canada	Confidential
28 Environment Canada	Dr Robert Slater, former senior assistant deputy minister
29 Essroc	Gary Molchan, VP Environmental Affairs
30 Forest Products Association of Canada	Avrim Lazar
31 Forest Products Association of Canada	Paul Lansbergen, Director, Economics, Energy and Climate Change
32 Gaz Métro	Confidential
33 Government of British Columbia	Confidential
34 Holcim Canada	Luc Robitaille
35 International Institute for Sustainable Development	John Drexhage, Director, Climate Change and Energy Program
36 ISC3 Secretariat	Confidential
37 Lehigh Cement	Brent Korobanik, Manager, Environment
38 Mining Association of Canada	Gordon Peeling, President and CEO
39 Mining Association of Canada	Paul Stothart, Vice President, Economic Affairs
40 National Round Table on the Environment and the Economy	David McGuinty, MP (Liberal environment critic), former executive director
41 Nexen	Wishart Robson, Senior Advisor for Climate Change
42 Natural Resources Canada	Confidential
43 Natural Resources Canada	Confidential
44 Natural Resources Canada	Confidential
45 Office of the Auditor General	Confidential
46 Office of the Minister of the Environment	Confidential
47 Office of the Minister of the Environment	Dahlia Stein, Senior Policy Advisor (Environment)
48 Pembina Institute	Marlo Raynolds, Executive Director
49 Pembina Institute	Matthew Bramely, Director, Climate Change
50 Petro-Canada	Confidential
51 Railway Association of Canada	Cliff Mackay, President and CEO
52 Shell Canada	Confidential
53 Sierra Club	Stephen Hazzell, Executive Director
54 St. Mary's Cement	Martin Vroegh, Environment Manager
55 Suncor Energy	Gordon Lambert, VP Sustainable Development
56 TransAlta	Robert Page, former vice president sustainable development
57 Union Gas/Spectra Energy	Julie Dill, President and CEO
58 West Fraser Timber	Cindy McDonald, Manager Environmental Affairs
59 Weyerhaeuser	Confidential
60 WWF/Boxfish Consulting	Lorne Johnson, former director of Ottawa Branch, WWF, and Consultant, Boxfish

Works Cited

Ackerman, B. 1985. "Toward a Theory of Statutory Evolution: The Federalization of Environmental Law." *Journal of Law Economics and Organization* 1 (2): 313–40.

Alvarez, P., and J. Dielwart. 2002. Letter to the Hon. Gordon Balser and the Hon. Chester Gillan, 18 November.

Arora, S., and T.N. Cason. 1996. "Why Do Firms Volunteer to Exceed Environmental Regulations? Understanding Participation in EPA's 33/50 Program." *Land Economics* 72 (4): 413–32. http://dx.doi.org/10.2307/3146906.

Barnard, J.W. 1991. "Institutional Investors and the New Corporate Governance." *North Carolina Law Review* 69:1135–87.

Battelle Memorial Institute. 2002. *Toward a Sustainable Cement Industry*. Columbus, OH: Battelle Memorial Institute.

BCNI (Business Council on National Issues). 1994. "Canada's business leaders outline a voluntary strategy to combat global climate change." *Communiqué*. Ottawa, 4 November.

Benn, S., D. Dunphy, and A. Martin. 2009. "Governance of Environmental Risk: New Approaches to Managing Stakeholder Involvement." *Journal of Environmental Management* 90 (4): 1567–75. http://dx.doi.org/10.1016/j.jenvman.2008.05.011.

Bernstein, S. 2002. "International Institutions and the Framing of Domestic Policies: The Kyoto Protocol and Canada's Response to Climate Change." *Policy Sciences* 35 (2): 203–36. http://dx.doi.org/10.1023/A:1016158505323.

Blackwell, R. 2009. "Nexen adjusts Long Lake plan." *Globe and Mail*, 10 December.

Bramley, M. 2000. *A Climate Change Resource Book for Journalists*. Calgary: Pembina Institute.

British Columbia. 2008. "BC first province to legislate cap and trade." News Release. Victoria, 3 April.

Brooks, S. 1989. *Public Policy in Canada: An Introduction*. Toronto: McClelland and Stewart.

Bruno, K. 1992. "The Greenpeace Book of Greenwash." London: Greenpeace.

Bulkeley, H., and M.M. Betsill. 2003. *Cities and Climate Change: Urban Sustainability and Global Environmental Governance*. New York: Routledge. http://dx.doi.org/10.4324/9780203219256.

Burtraw, D., and K. Palmer. 2004. "SO2 Cap-and-Trade Program in the United States: A 'Living Legend' of Market Effectiveness." In *Choosing Environmental Policy: Comparing Instruments and Outcomes in the United States and Europe*, ed. W. Harrington, R.D. Morgenstern, and T. Sterner, 41–66. Washington, DC: Resources for the Future Press.

Burrows, M. 2007. "Petro-giants will accept a carbon price." *Georgia Straight*. 5 December. Available online at http://www.straight.com/article-123594/petro-giants-will-accept-a-carbon-tax.

Canada. 2002a. *A Discussion Paper on Canada's Contribution to Addressing Climate Change*. Ottawa: Environment Canada.

Canada. 2002b. "Government of Canada releases climate change plan for Canada." Press release. Ottawa, 21 November.

Canada. 2005. "Notice of Intent to Regulate Greenhouse Gas Emissions by Large Final Emitters." *Canada Gazette Part 1* 139 (29): 2489.

Canada. 2008. Environment Canada. "Turning the Corner: Taking Action on Climate Change." Ottawa. Available online at http://publications.gc.ca/collections/collection_2009/ec/En88-2-2008E.pdf.

CAPP (Canadian Association of Petroleum Producers). 1999. *Upstream Oil and Gas Industry Options Paper: Report of the Oil and Gas Industry Working Group of the Industry Issues Table to the National Climate Change Secretariat*. Calgary: Canadian Association of Petroleum Producers.

CBC News. 2003. "TrueNorth Energy suspends oil sands project." 14 January. Available online at http://www.cbc.ca/news/business/truenorth-energy-suspends-oil-sands-project-1.393222.

CCCE (Canadian Council of Chief Executives). 2002. "The Kyoto Protocol Revisited: A Responsible and Dynamic Alternative for Canada." Ottawa: Canadian Council of Chief Executives.

CCCE (Canadian Council of Chief Executives). 2005. "Kyoto plan still does not measure up, say Canada's chief executives." Press release. Ottawa, 14 April.

CCCE (Canadian Council of Chief Executives). 2006. "Draft Memorandum for the Honourable Rona Ambrose. P.C., M.P. Minister of the Environment, Government: Framework for a 'Made-in-Canada' Climate Change Plan." Ottawa: Canadian Council of Chief Executives.

CCCE (Canadian Council of Chief Executives). 2008. "CCCE welcomes National Round Table report on reducing emissions of greenhouse gases." Press release. Ottawa, 7 January.

CCRES (Canadian Coalition for Responsible Environmental Solutions). 2002. "Coalition formed to advance 'made-in-Canada' strategy on climate change." Press release. Ottawa, 26 September.

Cheadle, B. 2008. "Expert panel calls for carbon tax to reduce greenhouse gases." *Canadian Press*, 7 January.

Clark, A. 2009. "Exxon chief backs carbon tax." *Guardian*, 9 January.

Coleman, W.D. 1988. *Business and Politics: A Study of Collective Action.* Montreal; Kingston, ON: McGill-Queen's University Press.

ConocoPhillips Canada. 2008. *2008 Annual Report.* n.p.

Crittenden, G. 2003. "Impacts from the Kyoto Accord." *HazMat Magazine.* February/March.

Cyert, R.M., and J.G. March. 1993. *A Behavioral Theory of the Firm.* Englewood Cliffs, NJ: Prentice-Hall.

d'Aquino, T. 1996. "Global Climate Change: A Strategy for Canada and the Environment." Notes for an address to the Annual Policy Conference, Canadian Industry Program for Energy Conservation, Toronto, 6 November.

Dhaliwal, H. 2002. Letter from the Minister of the Environment to John Dielwart, Chairman, Canadian Association of Petroleum Producers, 18 December.

Dillon, J. 2002. Testimony to the House of Commons Standing Committee on Industry, Science and Technology. Ottawa, 5 December.

Dillon, J. 2003. Testimony to the Standing Senate Committee on Energy, the Environment and Natural Resources. Ottawa, 3 April.

Dillon, J. 2006. Testimony to the House of Commons Standing Committee on Environment and Sustainable Development. Ottawa, 28 November.

Doern, B.G., ed. 1978. *The Regulatory Process in Canada.* Toronto: Macmillan of Canada.

Doern, B.G. 1996. "The Evolution of Canadian Policy Studies as Art, Craft, and Science." In *Policy Studies in Canada: The State of the Art*, ed. L. Dobuzinskis, M. Howlett, and D. Laycock, 15–26. Toronto: University of Toronto Press.

Droitsch, D., M. Huot, and P.J. Partington. 2010. "Briefing Note: Canadian Oil Sands and Greenhouse Gas Emissions." Calgary: Pembina Institute.

Ehrlich, P., and Anne Ehrlich. 1996. *The Betrayal of Science and Reason: How Anti-Environmental Rhetoric Threatens Our Future.* Washington, DC: Shearwater Books.

Encana Corporation. 2008. Annual Report 2008. Calgary.

Environics, *Environmental Monitor*, 4th quarter 1992.

Environics, *Focus Canada*, various issues.

Environmental Defense Fund. 2000. "Global Corporations and Environmental Defense Partner to Reduce Greenhouse Gas Emissions." New York: Environmental Defense Fund.

Field, B.C., and N.D. Olewiler. 1994. *Environmental Economics.* Toronto: McGraw-Hill Ryerson.

Fishlock, R., and M. Mercer. 2005. "Canada's Climate Change Plan: Cooling Us Down or Just a Lot of Hot Air?" [n.p.]: Blake, Cassels and Graydon LLP. Available online at http://www.blakes.com/english/publications/belb/april2005/climatechange.asp; accessed 6 July 2010.

FPAC (Forest Products Association of Canada). 2010. "Sustainable Solutions." Available online at http://www.fpac.ca/index.php/en/sustainable-solutions/; accessed 2 August 2010.

Freeman, A. 2006. Remarks to the House of Commons Standing Committee on Environment and Sustainable Development. Ottawa, 12 December 2006.

Frieden, J.A. 1991. "Invested Interests: The Politics of National Economic Policies in a World of Global Finance." *International Organization* 45 (4): 425–51. http://dx.doi.org/10.1017/S0020818300033178.

Garcia-Johnson, R. 2000. *Exporting Environmentalism: US Multinational Chemical Corporations in Brazil and Mexico.* Cambridge, MA: MIT Press.

George, A., and A. Bennett. 2005. *Case Studies and Theory Development.* Cambridge, MA: MIT Press.

Gourovitch, P.A. 1977. "International Trade, Domestic Coalitions and Liberty: Comparative Responses to the Crisis of 1873–1896." *Journal of Interdisciplinary History* 8 (2): 281–313. http://dx.doi.org/10.2307/202790.

Greer, J., and K. Bruno. 1998. *Greenwash: The Reality around Corporate Environmentalism.* Penang, Malaysia: Third World Network.

Gunningham, N. 2009. "Shaping Corporate Environmental Performance: A Review." *Environmental Policy and Governance* 19 (4): 215–31. http://dx.doi.org/10.1002/eet.510.

Gunningham, N., R.A. Kagan, and D. Thornton. 2004. "Social License and Environmental Protection: Why Businesses Go beyond Compliance." *Law & Social Inquiry* 29 (2): 307–41. http://dx.doi.org/10.1111/j.1747-4469.2004.tb00338.x.

Hall, P.A., and D.W. Soskice, eds. 2003. *Varieties of Capitalism: The Institutional Foundations of Comparative Advantage.* New York: Oxford University Press.

Hall, P.A., and D.W. Soskice. 2009. "An Introduction to Varieties of Capitalism." In *Debating Varieties of Capitalism: A Reader,* ed. B. Hancke, 21–74. Oxford: Oxford University Press.

Harrison, K. 1996a. *Passing the Buck: Federalism and Canadian Environmental Policy.* Vancouver: UBC Press.

Harrison, K. 1996b. "The Regulator's Dilemma: Regulation of Pulp Mill Effluents in the Canadian Federal State." *Canadian Journal of Political Science* 29 (3): 469–96. http://dx.doi.org/10.1017/S0008423900008209.

Harrison, K. 2007. "The Road Not Taken: Climate Change Policy in Canada and the United States." *Global Environmental Politics* 7 (4): 92–117. http://dx.doi.org/10.1162/glep.2007.7.4.92.

Harrison, K. 2009. "A Tale of Two Taxes: The Fate of Environmental Tax Reform in Canada and the Province of British Columbia." Paper presented at the Global Conference on Environmental Taxation, Lisbon, 25 September.

Harrison, K. 2010. "The Struggle of Ideas and Self-Interest in Canadian Climate Policy." In *Global Commons, Domestic Decisions: The Comparative Politics of Climate Change*, ed. K. Harrison and L.M. Sundstrom, 169–200. Cambridge, MA: MIT Press. http://dx.doi.org/10.7551/mitpress/9780262014267.001.0001.

Harrison, K., and W. Antweiler. 2003. "Incentives for Pollution Abatement: Regulation, Regulatory Threats, and Non-Governmental Pressures." *Journal of Policy Analysis and Management* 22 (3): 361–82. http://dx.doi.org/10.1002/pam.10137.

Hendriks, C.A., et al. 2004. "Emission Reduction of Greenhouse Gases from the Cement Industry." Paper presented to the Seventh International Conference on Greenhouse Gas Control Technologies, Vancouver, 5–9 September. Available online at http://www.wbcsd.org/web/projects/cement/tf1/prghgt42.pdf.

Henriques, I., and P. Sadorsky. 2008. "Voluntary Environmental Programs: A Canadian Perspective." *Policy Studies Journal* 36 (1): 143–66. http://dx.doi.org/10.1111/j.1541-0072.2007.00257.x.

Hoberg, G., and K. Harrison. 1994. "It's Not Easy Being Green: The Politics of Canada's Green Plan." *Canadian Public Policy* 20 (2): 119–37. http://dx.doi.org/10.2307/3552101.

Hofmann, K.P., ed. 2007. *Psychology of Decision-making in Economics, Business and Finance*. Hauppauge, NY: Nova Science Publishers.

Hornung, R., and M. Bramley. 2000. "Five Years of Failure: Federal and Provincial Government Inaction on Climate Change during a Period of Rising Industrial Emissions." Ottawa: Pembina Institute.

Howlett, M., and M. Ramesh. 2005. "Patterns of Policy Instrument Choice: Policy Styles, Policy Learning and Privatization Experience." *Review of Policy Research* 12 (1–2): 3–24.

Hubbard, D.W. 2009. *The Failure of Risk Management: Why It's Broken and How to Fix It*. Hoboken, NJ: John Wiley and Sons.

Hyndman, R. 2002. Testimony to the House of Commons Standing Committee on Industry, Science and Technology. Ottawa, 11 December.

ISC3 (Industry Steering Committee on Climate Change). 2002. "Synopsis and Action Items." Ottawa, 26 June.

Kincaid, J. 1996. "Intergovernmental Costs and Coordination in US Environmental Protection." In *Federalism and the Environment: Environmental Policymaking in Australia, Canada, and the United States*, ed. K.M. Holland, F. Morton, and B. Galligan, 79–102. Westport, CT: Greenwood Press.

King, G., R.O. Keohane, and S. Verba. 1994. *Designing Social Inquiry: Scientific Inference in Qualitative Research*. Princeton, NJ: Princeton University Press.

Kingstone, P.R. 1999. *Crafting Coalitions for Reform: Business Preferences, Political Institutions, and Neoliberal Reform in Brazil*. University Park, PA: University of Pennsylvania Press.

Klee, H., and E. Coles. 2004. "The Cement Sustainability Initiative: Implementing Change across a Global Industry." *Corporate Social Responsibility and Environmental Management* 11 (2): 114–20. http://dx.doi.org/10.1002/csr.59.

Knight, F.H. 1985. *Risk, Uncertainty, and Profit*. Midway Reprint ed. Chicago: University of Chicago Press.

LeBlanc, A. 1995. "No Sign of Consensus on Climate Change." *Canadian Chemical News*, 1 July.

Litfin, K. 2000. "Advocacy Coalitions along the Domestic-Foreign Frontier: Globalization and Canadian Climate Change Policy." *Policy Studies Journal* 28 (1): 236–52. http://dx.doi.org/10.1111/j.1541-0072.2000.tb02026.x.

Lizza, R. 2010. "As the World Burns: How the Senate and the White House Missed Their Best Chance to Deal with Climate Change." *New Yorker*, 11 October.

Lorenzoni, I., and N.F. Pidgeon. 2006. "Public Views on Climate Change: European and USA Perspectives." *Climatic Change* 77 (1–2): 73–95. http://dx.doi.org/10.1007/s10584-006-9072-z.

Macdonald, D. 2003. "The Business Campaign to Prevent Kyoto Ratification." Paper presented to the Annual Meeting of the Canadian Political Science Association, Halifax, NS, 31 May.

Macdonald, D. 2007. *Business and Environmental Politics in Canada*. Peterborough, ON: Broadview Press.

Macdonald, D., D. Houle, and C. Patterson. 2011. "L'utilization du volontarisme afin de contrôler les émissions de gaz à effet de serre du secteur industriel." In *Politiques environnementales et accords volontaires: le volontarisme comme instrument de politiques environnementales au Québec*, ed. J. Crête, 75–97. Montreal: Les Presses de l'Université Laval.

Macdonald, D., and H. Smith. 1999. "Promises Made, Promises Broken: Questioning Canada's Commitments to Climate Change." *International Journal* 55 (1): 107–24. http://dx.doi.org/10.2307/40203458.

Mansbridge, J. 1992. "A Deliberative Theory of Interest Representation." In *The Politics of Interests: Interest Groups Transformed*, ed. M.P. Petracca, 32–57. Boulder, CO: Westview Press.

Martin, K.J., and J. McConnell. 1981. "Corporate Performance, Corporate Takeovers, and Management Turnover." *Journal of Finance* 46 (2): 671–87.

McCarthy, S., and G. Galloway. 2010. "Ottawa stalls on emissions rules." *Globe and Mail*, 15 April.

Mickwitz, P. 2003. "A Framework for Evaluating Environmental Policy Instruments: Context and Key Concepts." *Evaluation* 9 (4): 415–36. http://dx.doi.org/10.1177/1356389003094004.

Milner, H., and D. Yoffie. 1989. "Between Free Trade and Protectionism: Strategic Trade Policy and a Theory of Corporate Preferences." *International Organization* 43 (2): 239–72. http://dx.doi.org/10.1017/S0020818300032902.

Morton, P. 1990. "Canadian oil industry relieved feared carbon tax omitted from 'green plan.'" *Oil Daily*, 14 December.

Nexen. 2008. Annual Report 2008. Calgary.

Nexen. 2010. Annual Report 2010. Calgary.

NRTEE (National Round Table on Energy and the Environment). 2007. *Getting to 2050: Canada's Transition to a Low-emission Future: Advice for Long-term Reductions of Greenhouse Gases and Air Pollutants.* Ottawa: National Round Table on Energy and the Environment.

Paton, R. 2005a. Letter from the President and Chief Executive Officer, Canadian Chemical Producers' Association, to the Hon. Stéphane Dion, Minister of the Environment, 5 January.

Paton, R. 2005b. Letter from the President and Chief Executive Officer, Canadian Chemical Producers' Association, to the Hon. Stéphane Dion, Minister of the Environment, 28 October.

Peeling, G. 2002. Remarks to the House of Commons Standing Committee on Industry, Science and Technology. Ottawa, 11 December.

Petro-Canada. 2008. *2008 Annual Report*. Calgary.

Pew Center on Global Climate Change. 2008. "Scope of a Greenhouse Gas Cap-and-Trade Program." Congressional Policy Brief. Arlington, VA: Pew Center on Global Climate Change.

Porter, M.E. 1985. *Competitive Advantage*. New York: Free Press.

Porter, M.E., and C. van der Linde. 1995. "Toward a New Conception of the Environment-Competitiveness Relationship." *Journal of Economic Perspectives* 9 (4): 97–118. http://dx.doi.org/10.1257/jep.9.4.97.

Powell, R.G. 1997. "Modelling Takeover Likelihood." *Journal of Business Finance & Accounting* 24 (7–8): 1009–30. http://dx.doi.org/10.1111/1468-5957.00148.

Power, M. 2007. *Organized Uncertainty: Designing a World of Risk Management.* Oxford: Oxford University Press.

Prakash, A. 2000. *Greening the Firm.* Cambridge: Cambridge University Press. http://dx.doi.org/10.1017/CBO9780511491863.

Rabe, B.G. 1999. "Federalism and Entrepreneurship: Explaining American and Canadian Innovation in Pollution Prevention and Regulatory Integration." *Policy Studies Journal* 27 (2): 288–306. http://dx.doi.org/10.1111/j.1541-0072.1999.tb01969.x.

Reilly, F.K., and K.C. Brown. 2006. *Investment Analysis and Portfolio Management.* Cincinnati, OH: South-Western College Publishing.

Rennie, S. 2009. "Tory Green Plan in for tune-up: Prentice." Canadian Press, 2 April.

Rogowski, R. 1987. "Political Cleavages and Changing Exposure to Trade." *American Political Science Review* 81 (4): 1121–37. http://dx.doi.org/10.2307/1962581.

Rowell, A. 1996. *Green Backlash: Global Subversion of the Environmental Movement.* London: Routledge.

Savoie, D.J. 2003. *Governing from the Centre: The Concentration of Power in Canadian Politics.* Toronto: University of Toronto Press.

Stern, N. 2006. *The Economics of Climate Change: The Stern Review.* Cambridge: Cambridge University Press.

Stuewer, S.K. 2008. Letter from the Vice President, Safety, Health and Environment, Exxon Mobil, to Janice Adair and Steven Owens, Co-Chairs of the Western Climate Initiative.

Suncor Energy. 2008. *2008 Annual Report.* Calgary.

Toner, G., and B.G. Doern. 1986. "The Two Energy Crises and Canadian Oil and Gas Interest Groups: A Re-examination of Berry's Propositions." *Canadian Journal of Political Science* 19 (3): 467–93. http://dx.doi.org/10.1017/S0008423900054524.

Tversky, A., and D. Kahneman. 1999. "Judgment under Uncertainty: Heuristics and Biases." In *Judgment and Decision Making: An Interdisciplinary Reader*, 2nd ed., ed. T. Connolly, H.R. Arkes, and K.R. Hammond, 35–52. Cambridge: Cambridge University Press.

VanNijnatten, D. 1999. "Participation and Environmental Policy in Canada and the United States: Trends over Time." *Policy Studies Journal* 27 (2): 267–87. http://dx.doi.org/10.1111/j.1541-0072.1999.tb01968.x.

Vogel, D. 1989. *Fluctuating Fortunes: The Political Power of Business in America.* New York: Basic Books.

Vogel, D. 1995. *Trading Up: Consumer and Environmental Regulation in a Global Economy.* Cambridge, MA: Harvard University Press.

Lightning Source UK Ltd.
Milton Keynes UK
UKOW04n0619091217
314039UK00007B/302/P